The God Experience

Return to the Source

Ken O'Donnell

Debbie Castle

Judy Johnson

Indian Edition 2024

Cover Layout Judi Rich
Original Cover Art Mariana Santos
Editing Teri Crawford
Interior Layout Ella Saarinen & Gitte Hulden

DEDICATION

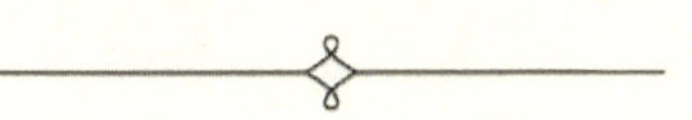

To our Beloved Source

TABLE OF CONTENTS

INTRODUCTION

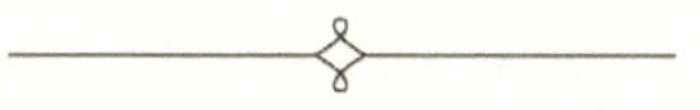

The question of God's existence has fascinated human beings ever since they started to ponder and later write down what was happening to them. The ancients depicted our world as one full of traps that take us away from the promise of a better life and spiritual development. Fear and threats were built into everything. The way around this was to propitiate the gods, remain devout and reverent in the hope that things would somehow become better. Adequate crops, sufficient rain, victory in battle - these were the signs that the gods were smiling.

Nowadays, the history of many traditions is in front of us. We can see that most of them try to reach out for something beyond the world of the five senses and its inherent materialism. Even though they believe in something beyond, many feel that there is no reasonable way to discuss what is loosely called the "spiritual realm."

The position of this book is that there is definitely a spiritual reality and that it has a similar coherent foundation for its existence as the physical one. This is particularly true related to God. People ask, "How can we prove that God exists when we cannot see spirit?" The modern world is so obsessed with the material that we can't seem to think about anything beyond it.

Interreligious Dialogue

Two of the main objectives of the Charter of Association of the Brahma Kumaris World Spiritual University Association are:

- To encourage the transformation of individual consciousness, attitude and behavior as the foundation of general progress in the human condition throughout the world
- To promote a better understanding of the global human family through understanding the spiritual connections between the world's religions.

These two objectives allow us to meet with other like-minded people and organizations that promote an understanding between religious and spiritual traditions. This has led to an appreciative exploration of these different beliefs and practices.

The very spirit of the ecumenical religious movement is the respect for plurality of beliefs. Under the umbrella of the inter-religious movement, all traditions come together to share experiences and understand similarities and differences without giving up their specific belief systems or philosophies, even when they are contradictory to each other.

Even though interreligious dialogue can sometimes be superficial, when it is real and profound, it serves as an antidote to many misunderstandings and prejudices. The hatred and killing we witness in the news have nothing to do with the deeper debate about God and God's connection with human souls. More than anything, we need to find common ground. This book is offered in this spirit.

Science, Religion and Blind Faith

Science has correctly rejected many superstitions inherited from our ancient past. Even so, there is still a lot of what is called blind faith about what God does and does not do.

On the other side, science has steered heavily

towards pure pragmatism, thereby creating its own form of blind faith.

There are two basic premises related to this:

> 1. Human beings can understand the universe in its entirety and science is the only means that can show the way. We eagerly await new discoveries that will, at some unknown future date, provide us with a full explanation of our existence.
>
> 2. The world that we see, hear, touch, smell, feel and measure is the only "real" world. People take birth, die and there is nothing else. Therefore, we think we may as well eat, drink and make merry as much as we can while we're here.

This type of thinking has encouraged a general preoccupation with the senses and their objects and an indifference to the things beyond them.

From Einstein, we know that time and space are inseparable, but where does the dimension of consciousness come into the way we see the material world? Everything that happens has a time and a place. And it also has a reason.

The Spiritual Dimension

It is in this dimension of consciousness that we can explore the spiritual realm, and everything related to it. This includes knowledge of the soul, God, the soul's relationship with God and the material world, and our existence beyond here. None of these aspects can be measured by any instrument of science, however sophisticated it may be.

We can understand the existence of the soul and God, but we can't really prove it in a way that would satisfy the logic of science. This does not mean that we must give up a rational approach to understanding God and God's importance. The major difficulty is that the experience of both the soul and God are completely subjective. We can only check spiritual matters in the laboratories of our minds and hearts.

This book not only states unashamedly that God exists as the source of all spiritual power and virtues, but also that we can interact with God in a way that deepens our understanding and experience.

If you have acquired this book it is because you believe in God's existence and you want to make sense of your relationship with the Divine. Moreover, you believe that with God's help, you can improve your life.

To explain the background to this book we can use the image of a bicycle wheel, with spokes spreading out from a central hub. At the end of each spoke, there are the many religious traditions. Each exists in its own right but obviously they are all connected to the same wheel of humanity.

If you travel back along any of the spokes, you come to the central hub of spiritual experience, which is common to all traditions. Here we find universal ideas about the spiritual realm including God. It is in this common territory that we share the very best of our humanity.

At the end of the spokes are the different languages and beliefs that generate confusion when we try to understand what others believe. The language in the central common space is the language of spirituality; silence and a love for the Divine that goes beyond words.

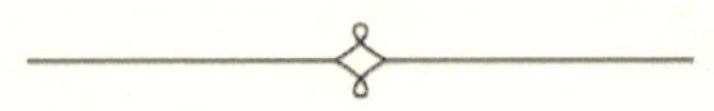

Access to God

All of the ideas related to God and our interaction with the Divine are connected to this common spiritual heritage that go beyond any particular tradition.

For the purpose of this book, it is useful to think of God as a Being, like us, a source point of energy, a soul; rather than a diffused, all-powerful energy field. Even if that soul, God, is Supreme in terms of spiritual power and qualities, as a Being, like us, God is totally accessible. This makes it easy to have a two-way conversation with God. God is neither male nor female, but a perfect blend of all the qualities we associate with the masculine and feminine.

This book is an invitation to open your mind and consider a new and more direct approach to interacting with God, without human intermediaries. With God as the Supreme Parent, we are God's children and have a right to claim our spiritual inheritance.

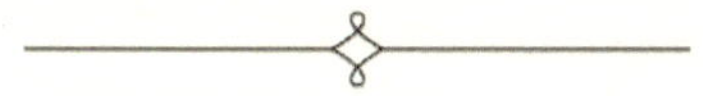

AUTHORS' EXPERIENCE

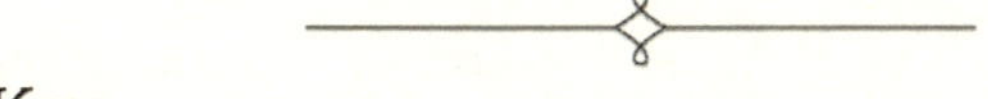

Ken

I have been a student of life and a constant world traveler since I was 21 years old. I have been to more than eighty countries and I have made it a point to understand the diversity of traditions on the ground. This love for the celebration of faith in the four corners of the planet began with a six-month overland trip from Australia, where I was born, to England. During this period, I experienced the main religious traditions of the world. I felt very old, but not particularly wise.

However, I was inspired to become a more spiritual person. I began to experiment with different kinds of meditation because I really wanted to enter my inner self and make the necessary repairs, if possible.

Despite the incredible variety of cultural perspectives that I witnessed; I began to realize that there was something consistent moving us as humans. I imagined that, through meditation, I could somehow come into contact with this common

territory where human beings really meet and that it was part of the depth of each one. I was deeply impressed by people everywhere making practically the same devotional gestures, just with different names and forms. Who are we really behind what we do and say? That was my big question.
After many great moments interspersed with many disappointing ones I decided, in my naivete, that I could discover these things if I could only get away from everything for a while. After about a year in England, I decided to go to the most exotic place nearby and chose Morocco for my personal research.

My idea was to spend six months in peace and silence contemplating the universe and my place in it. I had copies of the New Testament, the Dhammapada (the Buddhists' main scripture), the Bhagwad Gita, the Upanishads (dialogues between Yogic masters and their disciples) and the Koran. I would spend many hours daily meditating and reading these sacred texts.

Despite the idyllic conditions, I became more and more confused. I was not as detached as I thought. After five months, I decided that I had had enough, that I would not get any answers to the deepest questions about life by running away from it.

If there was any true spirituality, it would be something practical that was part of my work and relationships. I went back to London. Two weeks after I arrived, I made my first contact with the Brahma Kumaris from whom I learned about the Tree of Humanity and the Source.

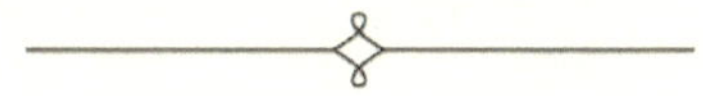

Debbie

I grew up in rural Canada, in a one-church community where everyone was expected to join as a teenager. For some reason unknown to me, at 10 years old, I decided I did not want to do this. I also said I wasn't interested in reading the Bible, which was a great surprise to my Dad who was a WWII veteran and had read it from cover to cover many times.

Later, as a young professional in education, I was introduced to values clarification as a way to bring personal enhancement into people's lives in the workplace. This values-orientation brought a 'spiritual approach' to my work in organizational development.

In 1999 I moved to Ethiopia to live and work, and a friend invited me to a yoga class. Dressed for a work-out, I arrived at the yoga centre to discover that the word *yoga* was being used to describe how, through meditation, one could connect with a higher power. And it happened just that way! As I sat in the mediation centre and had my first class on *Being a Soul* and *Connecting with a Higher Power,* I connected!

I think of that power now as God and this relationship has been a part of my daily practice and discipline for 20 years.

In 2001, I made my first visit to the headquarters of the Brahma Kumaris World Spiritual University in Mt. Abu India to attend the Peace of Mind Retreat with 100 others from around the world. We were immersed in the knowledge of Raja Yoga and the original qualities of the soul; peace, happiness, and love. It all made sense to me and through this introduction to the study, I became more aware of the wealth of knowledge within me awaiting discovery.

A year later, I returned to Mt. Abu and in a very special gathering, I heard God's voice in my head, say "I remember you." I have had an intimate connection with this loving Being ever since.

I am still happily learning and committed to living a peaceful lifestyle. Every day opens like a fresh blossom, full of beauty and appreciation, to be found everywhere.

To me, the precious relationship with God provides me with moment to moment guidance on how to maneuver myself in the world today. I have an appreciation of all the souls around me being my global brothers and sisters. I have a responsibility to be the best I can be and provide space for others to do the same. In this, God is a constant companion and guide.

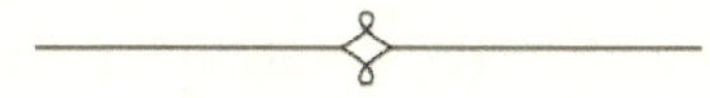

Judy

I have been working to make a better world since I was seventeen when I stayed for several months in a remote village in Asia as part of an international youth exchange. I witnessed first-hand the poverty and injustice of the world which lead me to get involved in social justice, community development and human rights work. As I *fought* for peace and justice, I noticed myself becoming angrier and less peaceful. There was a missing dimension to my approach.

On a business conference in Mexico, I had an unexpected experienced of bliss beyond anything I had ever experienced. I felt like I was beyond the awareness of this world. The experience opened a door in my mind. It was like the sun shining brightly in a place that had been dark. I felt like I was waking up. It changed my life and brought God as an intimate partner, friend, teacher, guide and loving parent. I have been so fulfilled in this primary relationship, there is nothing more I want.

As I stay close to God's pure energy, my inner world is changing; it is happier, lighter and more discerning. And I bring this energy into my relationships with friends, family and my work for betterment. I think of meditation now as *inner activism.*

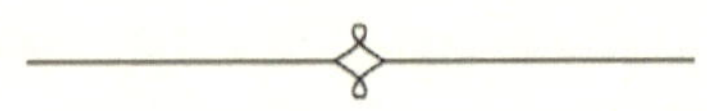

THE SEED AND THE SOURCE

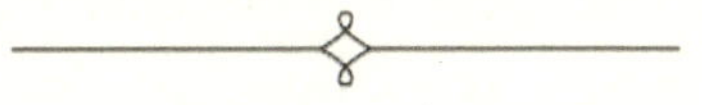

"In South Africa there is a treasured concept called Ubuntu *I am because you are.* I had been through a difficult period and was losing my faith in humanity. During a meditation workshop we experimented with taking light from God to transform ourselves. I experienced an incredible sense of freedom and joy seeing the sincerity of the other yogis. I felt us united by our connection to God. I know that I am safe in the hands of my world family because we are deeply connected to God, the Seed of the human world tree."

Devindree, South Africa

On the cover of this book, there is the image of a tree, which is perhaps the best representation of our human experience over time. It's like a spiritual photograph of world history. God is the Seed and the Source for the whole tree.

Each of the religious traditions is a branch of the tree. Each one is no better or worse than the other, just different. The trunk represents a time when the population was small and undivided. There was abundance, peace and happiness and therefore no need to search for the Divine.

Just as a physical tree grows and branches out, different branches started to appear on the tree of humanity. As the tree of humanity grew, each of the main religious traditions also developed its own branches and twigs. Human beings are the leaves that hang on the branch or twig of whatever they believe in.

Truth is not exclusive to any of the branches, rather truth lies in being able to see the whole tree. The tree shows us that we have a common heritage and explains the reason why we have similar aspirations.

The limitation of language makes it difficult to

describe deeper states of consciousness or even qualities such as love, peace and happiness. It seems that words have been invented to describe physical realities and we do not have a common language to adequately describe spiritual experience. When it comes to defining God and what God does or doesn't do, it's an even greater challenge.

We can look at what different traditions believe and what our own internal experience indicates. Even with this much, we can go into the depths of an experience with God. Meditation and communion with the Divine is a purely personal experience.

It is the right of every human soul to be able to have that connection with the One who is called the Father, Mother, Master, Guide and Highest Friend.

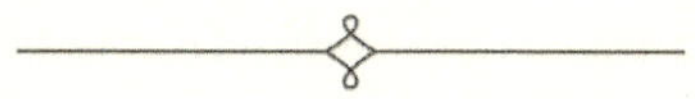

Similarities Amongst the Religions

Throughout history, organized religion has been influenced by culture and language as much as by divine inspiration. Yet the similarities among the religions are obvious; we are human beings who share this world together, and our trajectory has been similar. We are born in different places without knowing why.

We conjecture on the questions of where we came from and where we are going. We seek to be better and to avoid suffering and disappointment as much as possible.

We have bodies, traditions and languages with superficial differences, but at the internal level and in a very similar way, we appreciate virtues and beauty and we feel uncomfortable with defects and ugliness.

An Afghan mother, when she loses a child, feels the same as an American mother who goes through the same thing. A taxi driver in Buenos Aires is like his counterpart in Kuala Lumpur. They swear with different words, but they have the same meaning.

If we examine the world's major religions objectively, we can see differences and similarities, but always in the context of celebrating unity in diversity. We can observe the thread of humanity that passes through Hinduism, Buddhism, Judaism, Christianity, Islam, Sikhism, Taoism and others. The unfolding of these traditions has become the history of humanity itself.

They have many aspects in common - persecuted founders, the importance of sacred texts, prayer or meditation, as well as recurring themes such as "Love Thy Neighbor," compassion, spiritual development and individual responsibility for actions. The majority believe in one God.

We are too alike to make so much of our different interpretations of the divine dimension.

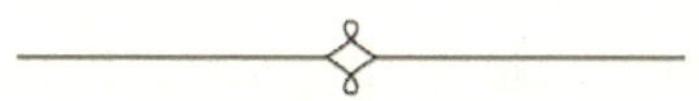

How Many People Believe in God (2019)

To answer this question, we consulted the free encyclopedia[1], which offers that 55.1% are monotheistic traditions, Christians (31.5%) or Muslims (24.6%). The next biggest group (15.2%) are those who are not affiliated with any major religion, half of whom, it is suggested, believe in God[2].

The fourth biggest group are Hindus (15%), who, even though they may worship different representations of the Divine, still refer to a Supreme One as Prabhu (Master), Ishwar (Supreme Being) or Paramatma (Supreme Soul). Many Hindus who are

---

1 https://en.wikipedia.org/wiki/List_of_religious_populations

2 https://www.adherents.com/Religions_By_Adherents.html

religious but do not worship a specific deity, refer to a universal God as Bhagvan.

If we include the Sikhs, Jews and Zoroastrians, we have almost 70% of the world population who believe in the existence of God.

Buddhists, with 7.7% of the world population, do not believe in a God or gods. Their focus is on spiritual enlightenment and a life beyond the forest of illusion (nirvana). Jains, Taoists and Confucianists also believe in the possibility of improving human behavior without a God figure.

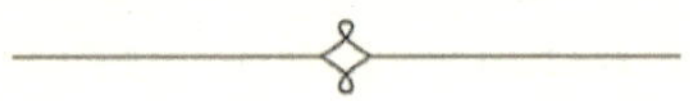

Different Beliefs about God

The main ideas that cover the spectrum of beliefs about God, the Divine or the Highest in the different traditions can be summarized as follows:

- Some do not believe in an Almighty Creator God but maintain the idea of the possibility of human perfection through spiritual effort, meditation and other practices.

- This is so in Buddhism. There is nothing in Buddha's teachings that suggests how to find God or worship the gods (from India). Although the Buddha himself was a theist (believing in gods because he was born a Hindu), his teachings are not theistic. He was more concerned with the human condition: birth, sickness, old age and death. The Buddhist path is about reaching a place of acceptance with these painful aspects of life, and not suffering through them.

- Some believe in non-duality, that God, a Divine Energy or a Creative Intelligence is present in every being and particle of matter, that everything is One.

    - One of the roots of this idea is the Advaita Vedanta School in Hindu philosophy. It postulates that the soul (Atman) is the same as the highest metaphysical reality (Brahman). This idea, which later came to be called omnipresence, states that what created all existence is also present and reflected in all beings and even matter, and that this creative principle was and is everywhere, always.

- Some believe that God became manifest through elevated human beings, deities, prophets or religious founders.
    - This is related to the idea that God incarnates on earth from time to time to eradicate the forces of evil, restore justice and free the worthy or the devout. One example is Vishnu who appears as Krishna to instruct through the Bhagavad Gita. In the same way, Buddha, Christ and others are considered by some as incarnations (avatars) of the Divine.
- Some believe in God as the literal Creator, Sustainer and Destroyer of all and everything, but remain separate as a reference for the rest of creation.
    - This idea of an all-powerful entity is supported by monotheistic traditions such as Islam, Judaism and Christianity. These believe that God's power is Absolute, that God created everything from nothing, that everything moves according to Divine will. Living beings are born, grow and die as part of that.

- Some believe that God the Supreme is separate from souls and matter, with different powers and functions, and thus remains a source of spiritual power for the rest of creation.

    - This is true of the Brahma Kumaris who study and practice ancient Raja Yoga, and adhere to the role of God as subtle, not literal. God does not create matter or souls, but periodically regenerates spiritual power in souls to help renew our world. It is this spiritual recharge of the battery of the soul that sustains creation.

    - The loving connection between souls and the Divine destroys all negativity and weakness within them. In other words, God's presence, knowledge and power are all spiritual.

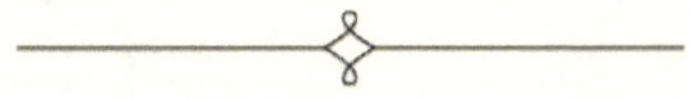

Common Ideas about God

Despite the variety of ideas about God, there is a fair amount of agreement, not only among the different faith traditions, but from the experience of our own hearts, such as:

- *God is a transcendental being.* This is why members of any tradition close their eyes to go beyond the material world whenever they pray to or meditate on God.

- *God is the benefactor for human souls.* We intuitively know that God exists to help us.

- *God is a source of spiritual power.* The closest parallel we have to God in this physical world is the sun, a source of light, as remembered in many traditions, especially ancient and indigenous ones.

- *God is light.* There has been an unceasing search for illumination in all traditions.

- *God is the source of spiritual wisdom and guidance.* This is the theme of so many hymns and prayers. When we have a problem, we expect God to give us the wisdom to sort it out.

- *God is the source of unconditional love.* Perhaps this is the reason for which we seek love in all our relationships.

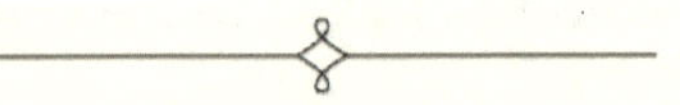

Religare - Reconnect with the Source

The word religion comes from *religare* which means to re-link, usually used in the context of God. No matter whether one has ever accessed God or not, most would acknowledge that the existence of that One is of a more subtle, non-physical nature than that of human beings. There is no scientific instrument or physical means to prove God's existence. We can only verify this through personal spiritual experience. Only then can we experience the transformative nature of the connection.

In Raja Yoga meditation, we mentally fly towards this spiritual sun we recognize as God, recharge our battery and begin to comprehend the depth of the relationships that are important for the soul - Parent-child, Teacher-student, Guide-disciple, Friend-friend, etc.

This is perfectly feasible because God is seen not as simply the source of highest spiritual energy but as the highest personality. God is a soul or spiritual being like me, but with superior qualities, making God easily loveable and accessible to all.

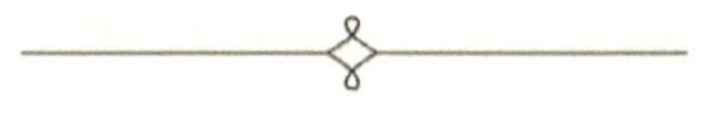

Raja Yoga Meditation

Yoga means union or the loving connection between the individual soul and God, the Supreme Soul, in order to recharge the spiritual battery and overcome negative tendencies that have accumulated. The connection itself implies the dual nature of our existence.

In other words, the human soul is not God. The One who is beyond change, therefore remains the Source of spiritual power and indeed is the only hope for a civilization whose systems are rapidly crumbling.

The practice of Raja Yoga, at its highest level, is the experience of a natural relationship with the Supreme Being. Therefore, it does not require specific rituals, physical postures or forced endeavours.

Using deep points of spiritual knowledge about the spiritual dimension beyond and about the form and attributes of both the soul and God, I can develop this union with a lot of love. It is love and not dry theory that makes this experience work.

Each soul can gather all their love and concentrate on God's essential form as a point of benevolent light, and soon begin to receive the return as an incredible current of bliss.

We ask you to be open to considering God as point of spiritual energy like the soul, except unlimited. The presence of the Divine can be experienced anywhere, which does not mean that God is present everywhere and in everything. The Supreme Soul exists in a different dimension to this physical one. To connect with the Source, we have to remember God with love and then we are able to experience God's qualities.

This is the approach we will be using in the meditation commentaries offered in this book.

How to Use This Book

These ideas presented here are based on teachings from the Brahma Kumaris World Spiritual University[3]. The chapters are related to a campaign that was held in our centres throughout the world during 2019, with focus on the general public as an audience.

---

[3] www.brahmakumaris.org

Each chapter has five parts:

- A brief introduction to the theme
- Personal experiences shared by young meditators around the world
- Personal exploration to take you into the depth of the theme
- Typical questions and answers related to the theme
- A meditation commentary to help you connect to the Source

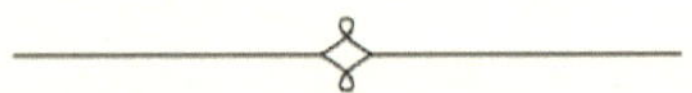

Five preliminary steps to all meditation commentaries

There are eight chapters in this book, each one describes a commonly held attribute of God shared by the many monotheistic faiths. The meditation commentaries in each chapter require some preparation.

Incorporate the five steps below as preparation for each meditation commentary to ensure you are in a receptive state to interact with the Source.

1. *Find a seat in which you can sit comfortably without interruptions. Inform the other members of your household that you are having some quiet time.*
2. *Sit with your back straight without being too rigid, take a few deep breaths and relax your body. Observe the moment and what is happening around you.*

3. *Read through the whole commentary aloud once and then begin again. Read each point aloud for best effect and reflect on it before going onto the next.*

4. *Become aware that you are the thinking, spiritual identity influencing your life. You are in the centre of everything happening around you, as well as in the centre of your life. Just feel how beneficial it is to remain in the centre, still and stable, even though many things are happening around you.*

5. *Just as you are sitting on the physical seat, sit mentally on your seat of command, a few centimetres behind the eyes, in the middle of the forehead. Remain as this conscious observer as you read the commentary once and then a second time.*

Personal exploration

We invite you to explore your relationship with God. We know that through childhood associations or on the seeker's path, you may relate to a certain divine quality of God, influenced by these formative experiences.

We suggest that you enter the experience of this book from a place that is most familiar to you. The eight qualities selected are used by many of the world's religious traditions to describe God. Although different names may be used in each language or tradition, the quality is inherently the same. Each quality has a chapter in this book.

We would like you to scan this short list and choose a quality as a starting point for yourself. And then choose the next most familiar to you, and the next and so on.

Please create your own order for experiencing the eight titles in this book from the *somewhat familiar* to the *less familiar.* For each of us, it is a unique journey to forge relationships with God based on our own path and who we are when we begin the journey back to the Source.

Take a few moments to review the list offered here and create your path from *known* to *less known*. The qualities of the Divine are:

- Love
- Benevolence
- Truth
- Mercy
- Peace
- Protection
- Liberation
- Power

Once you have your list, take a few minutes to reflect on your choices. Open a new journal for this journey and record your thoughts as you go ... to help you appreciate your journey in experiencing God.

Look at the order you have created as your reading list for this book and consider the following questions:

- What connection do you feel to the qualities of God you have selected as *most familiar*?
- How has God *shown up* for you with these qualities?

- How has God's invisible presence enabled you to see or experience these qualities?
- What do you appreciate about your experiences of God in your life so far?

Now choose three qualities in this book that you would like to explore further. As you continue your journey exploring old and new relationships with God, take time to write and share your experiences with others who are open to these conversations.

From our own experiences, this is not a time to debate or defend God's existence, rather it's a time to link the best of yourself with God as the unlimited Source of all divine qualities, powers and virtues so as to recharge your spiritual battery.

THE OCEAN OF LOVE

"I experienced God's loving vision hitting the core of me, seeing me as a valuable diamond and accepting me as I am. I felt God seeing me as I really am, through all the impure layers which are covering the real self. Tears of love ran from my eyes and I felt completely safe and secure."

Ella, Finland

Understanding God's Love

Love is one of the most misunderstood words that surfaces in our attempts to improve our relationships; with ourselves, with each other, with the world around us and with God. We can even say that it is the most important quality in our existence. We seek it out wherever we can find it and try to make the most of it when we seem to have it.

Since it is so central to us, our capacity to love and be loved is extremely vulnerable if we don´t really understand what it is or where it comes from. Spiritual love has nothing to do with the attached love that makes us vulnerable. Spiritual love is like admiring a flower in nature and attached love is like plucking the flower and putting it into our very own vase.

In the context of this book:

- Spiritual love is a basic quality of the soul.

- God is the Ocean of Love, an unlimited source of love, who can activate the pure love that is inside the soul and has been ignored or buried.

- God's love sustains the capacity to experience and give spiritual love.

God is a source of spiritual power with whom I can have a connection because of the similarity of our spiritual energy. God is also a Being with many attributes. If we can imagine a perfect Father, Mother, Teacher, Guide and Friend, we can come closer through a loving relationship with each of these roles.

As the perfect Father, God gives us the sort of love that can help us stand on our own feet. As the Mother, God's love nurtures and comforts us with whatever we need spiritually. As the Teacher, God's love is expressed in the teachings given for our own welfare. As an ever-present Guide, God's love is expressed in the concern shown when giving directions related to our spiritual journey. God's love as a Friend is experienced in the consistency of companionship, supporting us to keep our heads high and our feet firm.

Through knowledge I can create a link with God, but if only intellectual, it will not remain stable. Through understanding, I can build a bridge between the self and the Supreme, but it is only through love that I can cross it. Both knowledge and love are needed. If there is no knowledge, there is no bridge. Having only love leaves me on my side of the bridge, alone and unfulfilled.

With both knowledge and love, I can begin to experience the pure love for the One who is the essence of all relationships - the Mother, Father, Teacher, Friend, Guide and so on. Any relationship in which affection can exist, is possible between the soul and the Supreme Soul. Because of the subtle nature of meditation practice, a purely intellectual approach is inadequate because both the soul and God are "incorporeal." It's only love that can propel me towards that One and keep me connected in a concentrated way.

After all, God is the unlimited Ocean of Love. No matter how much we take, there is no end to God's love.

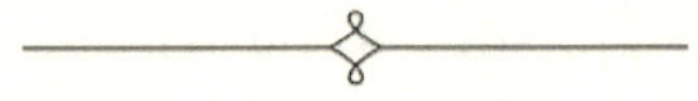

"My first powerful experience of God's love was feeling showered with a lot of love and feeling like a child belonging to the Ocean of love. No human being can give me that pure unconditional love. This acted as an engine that gave me so much power I could easily let go of attachment and expectations in my relationships."

Muna, Kuwait

Personal Exploration

1: Read these quotes about God as Love, taken from different religious traditions.

The Lord is our God; the Lord is one. You shall love the Lord your God with all your heart, with all your soul, and with all Your might.
(Judaism)

Whoever lives in love lives in God, and God in them.
(Christian)

There is a polish for everything that takes away the rust and the polish for the heart is the remembrance of God.
(Islam)

Leave your ego and go back to God - God is love. Lose your soul in God's love, I swear there is no other way.
(Sufi)

The Lord of the World is the Mender of the broken. He Himself cherishes all beings. The cares of all are on His Mind; no one is turned away from Him. ***(Sikh)***

My love is in thee, know it, that thou mayest find me near unto thee.
(Baha'i)

We call upon all that we hold most sacred, the presence and the power of the Great Spirit of Love and Truth which flows through all the universe to be with us and to teach us and to show us the way.
(Native American, Chinook)

Stop for a moment and reflect on which of these quotes resonates most for you. Write or share your thoughts.

2: Reflective Writing

Consider the following words used to describe God's love: ***unbroken, constant, unconditional and unlimited, makes me complete, pure, imperishable, true, altruistic.***

On a piece of paper, starting at the centre of the page, write outwards in spiral form towards the edge of your paper. Write your reflections about what is meaningful for you in these words and ideas about God's love?

3: Walking Meditation Commentary

Movement will play an important part in energy flow during this meditation. Read this commentary slowly aloud to yourself as you walk around the room.

As I walk, I reflect on my journey through life
I have been seeking
I have been searching
To find Truth
To find Love
While walking
I have wondered about God
I have wondered about true love
I prepare myself now
to experience God's love
I am ready
To experience it
I stop and stand still for a moment considering what it will be like
To experience God's love directly
Slowly, I return to my seat
And sit

As you sit, take a deep breath. And slowly read the following words aloud to yourself:

To My sweetest beloved child
you are the light of My eyes
you are Mine
and I am yours
Remember this always
~ God

Read it again then close your eyes and hold the words in your mind for a few moments in silence.

4: Reflection on the Ocean of Love

- What was your experience of reading the quotes, doing the spiral writing and the walking meditation?
- Why is it important to you to experience Divine love now?
- What will help you remember the true nature of God's love?

5: Embodying Divine Love

Each morning in your meditation, continue to connect to God's love in your own way. Take note of how the experience of God's love influences your day.

6: Meditation Experience

Take a few moments to read aloud and experience the following meditation commentary, beginning with the five preliminary steps (from page 36).

When finished, listen to any song that speaks of spiritual love. An example is: *What the World Needs*

Now by Will Young.

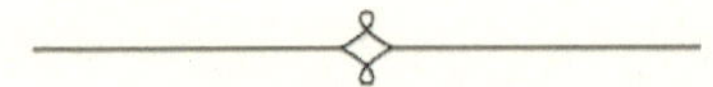

Meditation

I am aware of the world around me. At the same time, I am aware of the world within me.

As I synchronize myself, I become aware of my inner foundational state of love and reflect on that.

I remember its importance from my earliest moments in life. As a baby, I was nurtured by it. As a child, I was surrounded by it. As I grew up, I saw how my love expanded to include friends and other loved ones. I see how it comforts those who are at the end of their lives.

It seems that my whole life has been a story of loving and being loved, or a search for it when it was absent. Love has been at the core of my best experiences and my deepest yearnings.

This is because love is my natural, original state, that I have always referred to, both to give it and also to seek it. Of all of the lovable ones in the universe, I remember God, is the Ocean of Love.

I remember how God's love is an invisible force, always available to me, there to support me in both my darkest hours and my highest realizations.

I turn within, become aware of myself as a soul, a spark of divine light, centered, and still.

Using the power of my mind, I visualize a thread of thought energy, extending from the centre of my forehead behind the eyes and upwards.

Beyond the place where I am sitting, beyond my neighborhood and city, beyond my country and even this world. I visualize a place beyond the physical universe, which is not only my home but also God's home.

Mentally, I put myself in front of this wondrous source of spiritual light, a subtle sun radiating all God's qualities, especially love.

I am drenched by that unconditional love. I realize how much my experience in the physical world had been conditioned. This is now the true measure of what love can be.

Just as the sun shines continuously, without charging for its rays, I appreciate Your relentless love. It shows me how my love can be also.

Your love awakens my natural beauty and softens me, inspiring my highest feelings. Your love makes my own heart swell.

Your full acceptance of me destroys the distance between us as You remind me of my total importance.

You tell me I am good; I am pure; and I am worthy. I realize how much I am yours and You are mine as I bathe in Your love.

Just You and me and no one else. Just my exchange of love with You, sitting here with You.
I feel the unlimited love that You have for the world. You activate my love to serve humanity. The world is in front of me and with Your help, I radiate this love to the world.

Imbued with this deep experience of love from the Source of love, I slowly come back to my normal surroundings bringing Your love with me.

Frequently Asked Questions

Can God's love really be unconditional?

Only a Being who needs nothing from me can offer me unconditional love. Conditions are based on need or expectation. God has no expectations or needs, the way we, as humans do.

God's love is unconditional because God wants nothing from me. It is a one-way flow of pure energy from God to me. God does not take from me, only gives.

My love flowing back to God opens my heart and mind to receive more of God's love. We are together in an eternal relationship of love.

If God's love is equal for all, why are so many people born poor?

We are born into circumstances according to our own individual stories. Each of us has a unique part to play in this world drama and God does not determine who plays what part. God's love is independent of my social or economic status. In fact, for God, the most important thing is the quality of each one's heart or character. Over time it becomes obvious how the quality of a person's character determines the quality of their life.

If God really loved us all, why do young people die?

Young people, like the rest of us, die because things happen to their bodies, disease, disaster, accidents. There are so many manmade difficulties in our world today that people die suddenly and at a young age. God does not cause these deaths.

When a soul is connected to God, the death experience is an easing of the soul out of the body like a hair from butter. This departure is like moving towards the light.

THE BENEVOLENT ONE

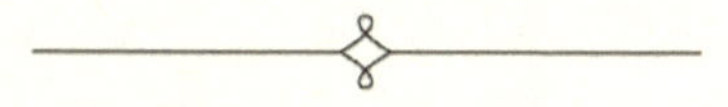

"Comforting light enveloped me for what seemed like an endless period during the moments after my mom died. It gave me so much strength that the whole next week I felt very light. It allowed me to share love and joy with all those around. Each time I remember the experience, it brings back tears of love."

Annie, USA

Benevolent and Benefactor

God is like the Sun. As the light of the sun shines 24 hours per day, God's benevolence is shining on us unconditionally. And as the earth turns away from the sun and the darkness creates night, so too, when we turn away from God, we feel disconnected from the Light.

Many of the ancient traditions likened God to the sun - always shining benevolently, making possible our lives on this planet by providing both light and heat. God of course, is not a physical sun but a spiritual one and radiates the Divine qualities of love, peace, happiness, purity and truth.

If we plant seeds away from the light of the sun, they cannot grow. If we hide ourselves away or distance ourselves from the light of God, we will not grow spiritually.

The word benevolence literally means the will to *do* good, just as benefactor means the one who *does* good. By comparing the basic beliefs about God in the different traditions, one can conclude that God is pure benevolence, shining a light to everyone and everything.

Something recorded in our hearts tells us that when

things are not going well and the shadows of sorrow fall on us, we can turn to the One who is our Benefactor. This instinctive turning towards the One beyond here, from whom we can receive the power and the understanding to overcome our difficulties, is present in all major traditions.

Even if we have no clear idea of God's form or place of residence, if things are getting tough, we can close our eyes, and reach out to the One Divine Power from whom we can receive benefit.

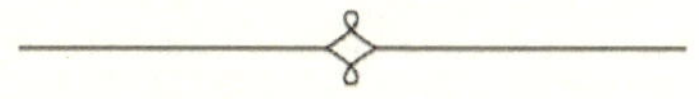

"I experience benevolence from God, that reminds me that God and I share the same heart. Like a teacher, by guiding me through life with teachings and company, I experience God's benevolence. I go through whatever difficulties may come, with flying colors. God's beauty is my beauty and God's light shines through my light nature giving love to all."

Roshni, Israel

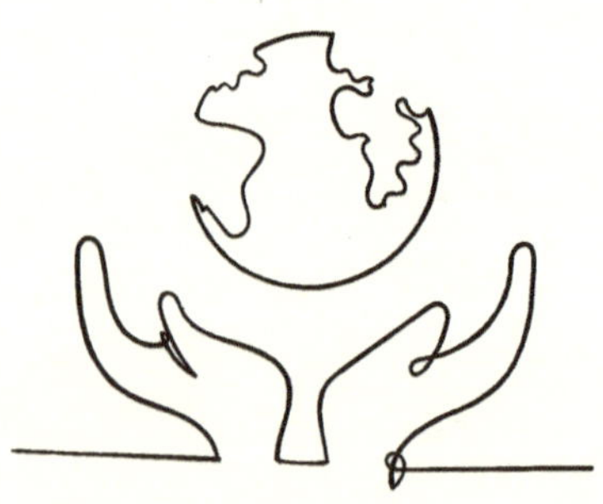

Personal Exploration

Benevolence is a word used mostly in relation to God. God's reputation comes partly from the experience people have of Divine benevolence.

1: Take a moment to reflect.

- What does benevolence mean to you?
  In times of abundance, people thank God for all that they have been given. In stormy times, people ask God for a sign to help them find their way. This is universal. Why?
- Why do all religions turn back to the same One?
- Why do people pray to God?

Even if people don't believe in God, there is a recognition of God in our daily language. *Oh My God* is a universal phrase used when we call out for help or when we are in awe.

- Why do we look to God for help?

Good-Bye comes from the ancient Scots when they left each other and said *God Be wi'yee (with yee)*

2: Parables of Goodness

The core message of each religion is goodness. There are parables and stories in all traditions that remind us of goodness. Fairy tales and pagan fables always have a moral.

- What stories or parables of goodness do you know? From what traditions?
- Re-tell yourself or share in conversation one of the earliest 'goodness' stories you know.

Take a moment to consider:

- What do these stories tell us about God's Goodness or Benevolence?
- What are some characteristics of God's benevolence?

3: Short Commentary

Read this commentary aloud about the Seed of Goodness:

God as the Benevolent One
is the seed of goodness for humanity.
God is a seed of goodness.
Such goodness always gives.
God is only goodness.
God is a giver of well-being or wellness only.

God gives happiness never sorrow.
What is in the seed is in everything that grows from the seed.
When the seed is full of goodness, then its growth is also full of goodness.
As the Benevolent One, God is the Bestower who never takes, only gives.
Remembering God makes my goodness emerge.

4: **Core Message of Religion**

All religions have a core message of goodness, directing humans to be good, to act with virtue and kindness towards their neighbour. There is a seed of goodness in every religion's beginning. This goodness shone forth in such a way that people who encountered it thought: "This is something I want, I need...this is a message the world needs now."

Read these versions of the Golden Rule from a variety of religious traditions.

Buddhism

Hurt not others in ways that you yourself find harmful (Udana-Varga 5:18)

Christianity

Therefore, all things whatsoever ye would that men

should do to you, do ye even so to them: for this is the law and the prophets.
(Matthew 7:12, King James Version)

Confucianism
Do not do to others what you do not what them to do to you.
(Analects 15:23)

Hinduism
This is the sum of Dharma (duty): Do naught unto others which would cause you pain if done to you.
(Mahabharata, 5:1517)

Islam
None of you truly believes until he wishes for his brother what he wishes for himself.
(Number 13 of Imam Al-Nawawi's Forty Hadiths)

Judaism
What is hateful to you, do not to your fellow man. This is the law: all the rest is commentary.
(Talmud, Shabbat 31a)

Native American
Live in harmony, for we are all related.

5: **Reflect** for a moment on these quotes and consider: What helps you stay connected to your goodness?

6: Meditation Commentary

Prepare to meditate with the 5 steps from page 36. Then read the meditation commentary slowly aloud to yourself. Sit in silence for a few moments and experience the energy of goodness and the Seed of Benevolence.

Meditation

As I reflect on myself and the state of the world around me, I feel a stirring inside to become the best me that I can be.

I imagine myself far away from the world and I can observe this tiny globe is just a beautiful tapestry of greens, blues, browns and whites. A tiny pearl swimming through space. Let me give my best feelings towards it.

As I come closer and look at the world directly around me, I am aware of how much help it needs. I reflect on how much I can be an instrument of benefit for the world. How can my own goodness be activated in order to help it?

This world, once brilliant and clean, has gradually

become darker. As the light of the souls becomes dimmer, there are some individuals whose light stands out in order to give any guidance that they can.

People of goodwill everywhere meditate and pray in order to make the world a better place.

I go within and become aware of my core of basic goodness yearning to come out and help in this task.

I see myself as a spiritual being, mentally set on my seat of command, caught between these inner stirrings and the world around me that needs help.

Stable in this consciousness I remember my connection with the Source of all spiritual power, the one we call God, Allah, Jehovah, Shiva, the Great Spirit and many other names. I become especially aware of God's role as the Benefactor for all.

Even the founders of the major religions were aware that there was a Source of Benefit beyond this physical world, to whom they also turned their thoughts when in deep need of help.

The heroes of the human world are the ones whom we feel have helped most, but Who or What was helping them?

I leave the world and its varied stories behind and I send my thoughts to that region of light remembered of old as Heaven, Nirvana, the Land of Peace. It is just my sweet home, where I was before I came onto this physical world, the ultimate reference for silence and stability.

It is not just my home, but the home of the One Source, my spiritual Father and Mother. My thoughts fly to that Presence.

I do not see any human figure, but a subtle sun-like being, radiating spiritual light and power.

I am aware that this One is pure benevolence. The rays of that benevolence flow over and through me, stimulating the core of goodness which is at the centre of my being.

Seeing the whole picture of the ups and downs of history, I become aware of how everything that has happened has been the playing out of the laws of balance. Everything and everyone could only do what they had to do.

I see the condition of the present world and know deeply my default position towards everyone and everything is one of benevolence – the same benevolence that my Spiritual Father emanates.

I bring the tiny globe of our world in front of me.

Internally I am connected up with the Source of Benevolence, and I become an instrument to shine that benevolence into our world.

From a distance I cannot see any individual or collective story. I am just aware that the energy that can best help is pure benevolence.

By aligning myself with God's Benevolence my true vocation to serve others is ignited.

I remain in this awareness for a few moments longer and gradually come back to my surroundings.

Listen to a song such as *You Raise Me Up* by Josh Groban (or any uplifting song in your language that speaks to God's benevolence making you rise to your best).

Frequently Asked Questions

I hear that we are all God's children and God loves us all equally. If this is true why are we not given the same resources to live this life?

Each of us is born into different circumstances. As a Spiritual Parent (Father and Mother), God loves all children equally even if each child has a different story and different capacity. God encourages each child to be resilient, to make the best use of the internal and external resources available to them. If a child does not use these resources well, they lose them. God does not give or take material resources from us. We use or misuse the resources we have, then we have less.

When we receive something by surprise, that I wasn't expecting, does this mean it came from God?

The sweet spiritual surprise of a sudden unexpected feeling of good will, clarity or power may be a flood of pure energy coming from God. The more I stay close to God's pure energy, the more I will draw it close to myself. Then in unexpected moments, I will feel God's presence as a sweet surprise.

I want to give back to God for all the Divine blessings given to me in this life, how do I give back to God?

God needs nothing, so there is nothing I can give to God. However, God loves an honest, pure heart. The best way to express my love and appreciation to God is to spend time in mental conversation with God as my companion during the day's activities and to give my burdens to God. The best thing I can do for God is take care of my mind and heart, so they remain free from the negative aspects that bind me to sorrow. Then I can stay close to God's loving protection and bring the energy of goodness to others.

GOD AS TRUTH

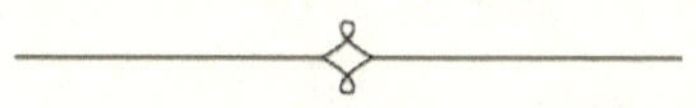

"I experience TRUTH from God like a beam of healing light. This light frees me from comparison, because God's Truth reminds me of my unique and humble nature. Then, I don't compromise myself, or impose my ideas on others. I am free to let go of various arguments and let life take its wise course."

Maria, Greece.

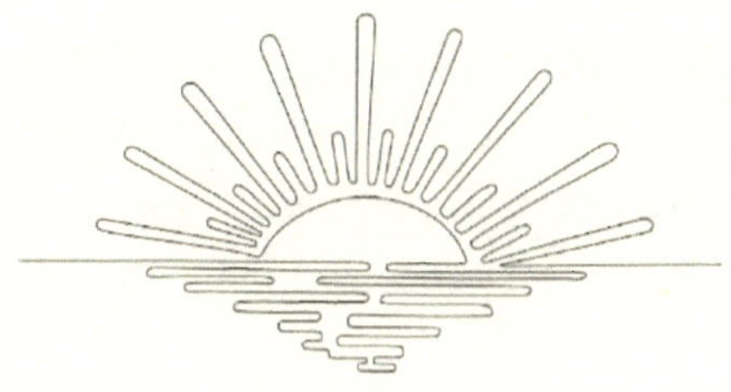

The Source of Truth

One of the greatest paradoxes is that we think, think, think in order to get the clarity we need to not think anymore. We speak, speak, speak with ourselves and others so that when we reach clarity, we don't need to speak any more. We do, do, do in order to not have to do anything anymore because we have built what we had to build.

The search for clarity and a sense of control in our lives indicates the deep need for real truth. We search for it in the remnants of lost civilizations, in the sacred texts of our traditions, in the depths of the ocean and outer space. Is there a satisfactory explanation about why we exist, where we are from and where we are going?

As a living, conscious Being, God is the Seed of the human world tree, and knows, how, what and why everything happens in the way that it does. God understands the full process through which we have passed.

At some point in the past, we came onto this physical plane and left our spiritual home where God is the main resident. We came here to play our respective roles through our body-costumes and forgot this original connection. By forgetting our spiritual identity, we also moved away from our innate qualities of peace, love, happiness, purity and truth, which are also God's essential qualities.

What has always been true about who we are and what we are doing, is recorded in us. Because of the pressure and chaotic nature of external circumstances, we move away from our central core which contains our spiritual reality and start to look for those qualities outside of us - in Nature, in other people and even in the technological gadgets our cleverness produces for us.

God, however, has never moved away from the original state and Divine qualities. God is the only unaltered Being in the universe. In that changeless state, the Supreme remains as the mirror in which we can see our real selves, and also measure the extent of each quality.

The truth of that measure tells us intuitively if someone or some situation has true love, or true peace or true happiness. While the false forms of these qualities dance around us and generate illusions, there is something deep in our core that tells us if something is true or not.

By connecting with God, as the Source of Truth, we can align with what is best in us, and have the strength to move away from what is not.

By keeping God's company, I can also enjoy the truth that is behind every person and circumstance, no matter how difficult or adverse. Truth is in the depth of the story of souls and matter. God never forgets that reality. If I remain with the Divine, I can also see it.

God sees me the way I truly am, beyond my physical form and the roles I play in life. Whenever I forget my authentic nature, God is there for me with gentle reminders to advise, warn and explain to me the importance of staying faithful to myself and using my eternal potential for the benefit of myself and others."

Oldoez, The Netherlands

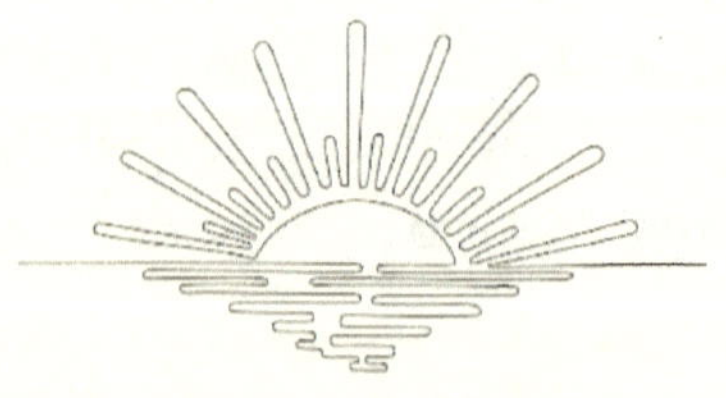

Personal Exploration

1: Select a Random Object

Look around where you are sitting now and select an object randomly. Take it into your hands. Please select an object before reading on.

Now consider for a moment in silence:

- What does this object reflect to you about your truth? Take a moment to make an association between the object and a truth about yourself. For example, perhaps you chose a teacup, which reflects your inner truth of comfort or contentment.
- What is the connection between your innermost qualities and truth?

2: Reflect on your own life experience and answer these questions for yourself:

- How do you know when someone is telling you the truth?
- How do you know when someone is lying? Or hiding something?

3: Read the following ideas and reflect on your thoughts.

- Facts: from the Latin *facer* means *to make*.
  Even indisputable facts have, at some point, been made and can be unmade. Facts reside at the level of the sense organs; what is seen, heard, tasted, etc. Facts are different depending on the perspective of the individual. This is why police gather multiple facts (perceptions) to find the *truth.*

- Truth is a vibration that lies deeper than facts or any interpretation of facts.

- Truth is energy ~ not words on a page. Truth is a deep, subtle vibration that can only be accessed through silence. Although beautiful words or music may act as a catalyst to awaken the feeling, truth is so profound that it can only be accessed when I turn my awareness inwards, away from the sense organs to the still point within. It is here, behind the words and feelings, that I find silence. Here I can also find the Divine. When I access silence, I can access truth.

- And consider more thoughts about truth:

  Truth endures over time.

The backdrop to everything is truth.

There is a truth behind our shared humanity that is crying out to be recognized.

There is a basic truth in our existence seen in the similarities of the religions.

The truth of humanity is not in our differences, it can be found in the similarities.

4: Explore the vibration of truth.

Consider the word pairs below and select one of the two words with the highest vibrational energy. Then explain to yourself why you chose the word you did (e.g. it felt deeper or more enduring or positive).

Beautiful	Pretty
Praising	Flattering
Blunt	Candid
Determined	Stubborn
Formal	Civil
Spontaneous	Impulsive
Dependent	Reliant
Striving	Driven
Enabling	Allowing

Word list taken from Hawkins, D. (2002) Power vs. Force

Reflect: What did you notice in your experience of discerning the vibration in the words?

This exercise can feel a bit like a mental workout. Our intellects have been refined to detect the difference between very subtle vibrations. The most difficult aspect is to explain why the word was chosen. We can discern truth without knowing how to explain our knowing because it is very subtle.

Most people, even in different cultures, select the same words:

beautiful - deeper, more enduring
praising - free from selfish motive
candid - honest without aggression
determined – positive
civil - deeper character
spontaneous - positive not reckless
reliant - more powerful
striving - forward positive
enabling - adding power

Even if you selected another word than the one above, what does it suggest that most people select the same words?

5: Consider:

- What are the qualities of God that make people refer to God as Truth?

The vibration of God is the highest vibration. And it resonates with the highest vibration (truth) in you. God as a Source of truth interacts with your deepest truth.

The language of God is not Portuguese, Hindi or English. It is the language of silence. What can you hear when you enter silence?

6: Preparing for Meditation

Take a moment to prepare yourself (page 36) to meditate. Sit in silence and contemplate the highest vibration in the universe - God. Then read this meditation commentary aloud to yourself.

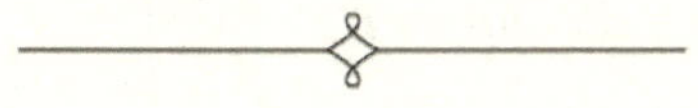

Meditation

I go within as I reflect on the nature of truth. At the surface of everything there are ups and downs, possible misinterpretations and mixed messages. But at the deepest level there are the basic truths upon which all is based.

We are spiritual beings going through a human experience. We are all children of the One Source called God.

As we play our parts in this physical world, each of us has our own process and story.

Physical matter, time and space do what they have to do.

We start off in our home of light beyond the physical universe, where we are silent, latent, conscious energies, ready for our manifestation in this physical world.

We start off pure, powerful, loveful, peaceful and happy. We are real and therefore true.

As we go through the scenes and situations of our stories here, we become distant from our original truth.

I let silence fill my mind and rest for a moment in the truth of my existence and my connection with the Source of Truth.

I feel my pulse of peace, my eternal spiritual heartbeat as I enjoy the language of silence, God's language. This is the portal for me to return to my truth. I become aware of God's eternal view of me. I ask, what do You see?

I feel Your highest vision on me, activating the deep spiritual truths which are recorded in me. This allows me to go beyond my present situation and details as You show me the breadth and depth of me.

As I sit with You, I begin to see the qualities that run deep and true within me, that have always been there, especially in the hard times.

My heart swells to see my truth and how beautiful it is. I remember how you are the only One who shines the light on my truth.

With Your help, I see beyond the veils of the adversity and privilege, beyond the façades of happiness and sorrow, beyond the guises of love and animosity.

In this state of being beyond, I glimpse the unseen secrets that my life's journey holds for me. I affirm the wonder of me.

I realize that I have been sometimes consciously and other times deliberately, seeking to return to this

perception of truth which is my essence.
In silent appreciation of the light of your Truth, I absorb and retransmit vibrations of truth to the world like a tiny lighthouse.

I remain in the joy of this experience some moments longer, and gradually come back to my present surroundings.

Frequently Asked Questions

How can I believe in God's Truth if I can't even see God?

God's truth is a concentrated pulse of pure energy. It comes into the mind and fortifies my will, my focus, my courage, my strength, my peace, my love. Whatever is needed in the moment is fueled by God's true energy. Then I am able to face, tolerate, support, accommodate, discern and decide with ease. When my truth is awakened by the vibration of God's truth, it enables me to bring benefit to others by making me feel so secure that I can share these vibrations. This increases the capacity and generosity of my heart.

If God is Truth, why do so many people of science have a difficult time believing in God?

Many scientists attribute their deepest insights and finest inventions to a Divine Source. Science has focused primarily on studying the material world. God cannot be found in the physical. Quantum physicists are beginning to understand the effect of energy on everything in the material world, as the space that exists between the particles. This is where we can begin to detect the effect of the human spirit and God.

However, because science considers consciousness to be an extension of the material brain, we are looking in the wrong place to find the truth of God.

How or where do we find God's truth, when there are so many prophets, priests, preachers saying different things about what God said and did?

Truth is a vibration that is recognized. We know when something is false because it doesn't *feel* right. In the same way, we can feel the rightness or wrongness of something if we pay attention to our conscience.

Ultimately, no matter what the moral code of the day, it is my conscience that will tell me what is true. I access my conscience by checking in with myself in silence. A clean conscience vibrates with truth and connects me to God.

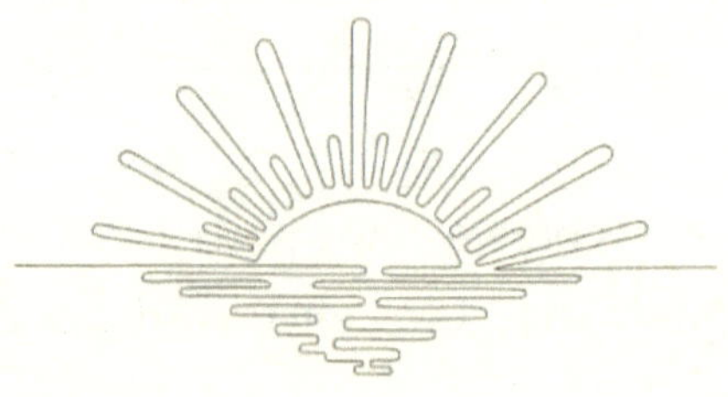

THE MERCIFUL ONE

"I experience mercy from GOD in the form of acceptance of who I am currently; the flaws and mistakes I have made. Despite feeling regretful and sometimes disappointed in myself for the mistakes made, I still experience love and comfort from God that makes me feel hopeful and positive about my future."

Vino, USA

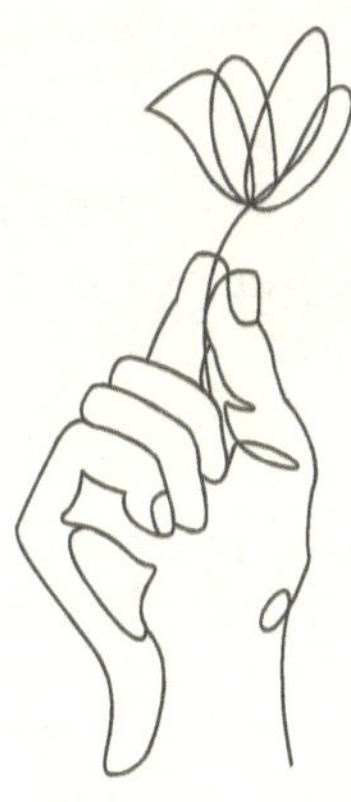

The Source of Mercy

The origin of the word *mercy* is connected with the pardoning of a debt - probably due to its Latin root *merx,* which means merchandise.

The idea that we need to get out of karmic debt, which is called *sin* in many traditions, leads us to ask God for mercy. In other words, we ask to be pardoned, because we can't sort it out for ourselves. The phrase, "O God have mercy on the soul" occurs in the prayers of the faithful of many traditions.

There is an implicit feeling that only God knows the full story and therefore, is the only One who can help us out.

Today, the meaning of mercy as *pardoning* an offender has changed to *compassion* for those who are in distressing circumstances. It is the loving concern that we have for others and ourselves, so that we can quickly get out of our difficulties and back on track.

The word *compassion* is even more revealing. It literally means to suffer with (*pati* in Latin) with (*com*). Divine compassion does not mean that God suffers with us, but that the cause of our suffering is understood by God.

We don't go back to the Source of Mercy to be pardoned, but to take strength and clarity so that we can understand the root causes of any suffering we may have.

Complete compassion would require us to have a full understanding of the circumstances surrounding our distress. This means we would have a vision of the past, present and future of the distressed person, even when it is myself.

Since only God has the full panoramic view of whatever we have been going through, only God can be totally compassionate and at the same time absolutely altruistic.

God's greatest mercy is not to pardon us from any wrongdoing, but to help us see things so clearly that we don't fall into these traps again.

Indeed, for real mercy, we need to come face-to-face with the One who is the Source of Mercy and have the courage to deal properly with the consequences of our own ignorance.

True mercy is also connected with the selfless

service of others. The highest charity is to help someone stand on his or her own feet.

Real spiritual service is to help someone sit on their seat of self-respect, to such an extent that they can decide with clarity what they want to do with their lives.

By staying in connection with the Source of Mercy, we are able to accurately feel the needs of others.

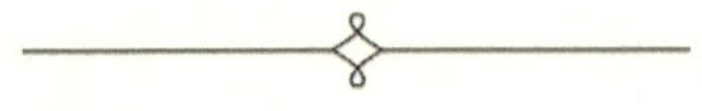

"I have tried every trick in the book to overcome my most difficult bad habits. I have punished myself, tormented myself, been angry, etc. but none of it ever helps. The only thing that seems to work is unconditional love for myself. God's mercy is that no matter how many times I fail, God's love for me stays intact. This mercy leads to true transformation."

Kristoffer, Denmark

Personal Exploration

1: God's mercy is so pure it doesn't need to be filtered; it is pure compassion. Think of a time or situation when someone had compassion for you.

- Describe the experience. Take a moment in silence to reflect, remember and write or share about the experience.
- Based on this experience write about your understanding of mercy and compassion.

2: People, things and situations mature over time. Just like fruit ripening over time, there comes a moment when it is perfect to eat. This is the same for our life lessons, situations occur for us to learn.

- Remember a mistake you have made in your life and when looking back now, you can see (with some detachment) that you learned something or that it was for the best. *"I know that was bad, but if it hadn't happened, I would never have learned about ____."*
- Write down 3 mistakes you have made. Look at them and consider what was the learning that

came from each mistake. How has time and distance revealed perspective and wisdom?

Mercy is an expression of the awareness that every situation brings lessons that mature over time. In this way I am spared from reacting prematurely to judge a situation until it has had time to mature. This enables me to have compassion and mercy, allowing myself and others to learn and grow from mistakes.

3: Consider the dictionary definition of mercy:

- compassion or grace shown towards someone, a feeling of sympathy for someone stricken by misfortune.

- to show understanding and to be gracious (graceful) in the face of someone's suffering

- an act of kindness, compassion, or favor

- leniency (as in a court of law)

Given these definitions, consider for a moment: Why would God be associated with the quality of mercy?

- God knows me better than I know myself. Because of this, God's love gives me unlimited chances to improve and doesn't step away from me. God is always a support in my desire to improve. This is God's mercy.

- When I access the Source, I receive power that I can use as courage and strength to become better.

- If I really understand myself the way God understands me, I will forgive myself. I will be compassionate to myself. God's mercy shines a light on the best in me so I can be myself and learn from my mistakes rather than beat myself up with self-criticism.

- In many religions receiving God's mercy is considered a right. God's mercy comes in the form of understanding and empowers us so we can steer clear of sorrow in the future.

4: Reflect on any insights you had about mercy and God as the Merciful One. Prepare for meditation (page 36) then read this commentary aloud to yourself. Then sit in silence for a few moments to absorb the experience.

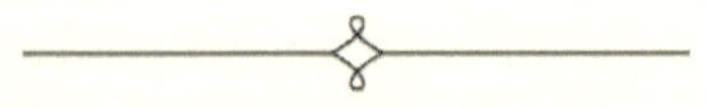

Meditation

I feel the world of people, technologies and systems pulsing around me at its frenetic pace. I know how much I have been caught up in it. In spite of this pace, I know that the answers are within me.

As a detached observer, I feel an incredible sense of relief, that I can sit stably within and enjoy my own qualities of peace, love and contentment.

From this deep sense of inner truth, I can even distance myself from the games of the ego running after comfort, identity, respect or even fame.

I am the master of all the many roles, relationships, responsibilities and routines. I see and understand all this.

I remain in this space of my true identity, having respect for what I am, as a soul, a child of the Supreme Soul. I am reminded of the power of this connection.

As mercy flows from understanding, I can have mercy for the persona that I play out in my daily life.

From this inner state, I can send good wishes to the set of personality traits that I have become.

I can even love my activities and connections in the physical world and keep the inspiration to become the best me that I can possibly be.

I embrace myself for what I am. I am grateful for the abundant life that is my stage here in the great play of time and space that is our world.

I know how I've been caught up in the intricacies and complications of my parts in the world. I know that the real me is not that, but a spiritual being behind them.

Because I know, I love. I can see others in their spiritual identities as souls and send them that love. This is the essence of compassion and mercy.

I am reminded of the One Source of mercy. God's mercy is unchanging because God never loses awareness of Self, of who and what God is or who and what we are.

On the screen of my mind, I see this wonderful, subtle, spiritual sun as the Source of spiritual life.
As I connect with that One, I feel Divine warmth wrapping me in love and acceptance.

God leads me back to my original state of peace, love, contentment, purity and truth. I remain deeply in the significance of this state.

I feel my highest potential bursting forth like petals opening to receive light and might.

They spread and spread, extending out into the world, to bring wounded hearts and confused intellects into the embrace of the Merciful One.

With my vision turned inwards and upwards, I see God. With my vision turned outwards to the world, I see my brother and sister souls in varying states of toil and hope.
I connect with the Supreme Source and like a tiny lighthouse, shining through the middle of my forehead, I become an instrument to send Divine rays of Mercy and compassion to everyone and everything.

If I could heal the world with one thought, it would be this.

With the comfort of knowing that I can come back to this state again and again, I gradually come back into the sweet silent atmosphere of the room.

Frequently Asked Questions

If God is all merciful, why doesn't God stop the pain and suffering in the world?

It is almost impossible to imagine a loving God not intervening to stop the pain and suffering in today's world. Pain is of the body and suffering is of the spirit. God gives comfort to the spirit, enabling us to overcome the pain and difficulties we face, but God cannot intervene to stop our pain. We must use God's power to overcome our difficulties.

If I am not willing to forgive myself, why should God?

When the soul is empty, mistakes are made. When I don't have the power to do the right thing, I do something that causes sorrow to myself or another. This sorrow accumulates over time. I am not to blame for becoming empty, it is a natural result of living. However, I will experience the natural consequences of the mistakes I have made. God cannot undo the mistakes I have made, but God can give me strength, hope and humility to face all consequences with dignity.

I'm the only one who needs to forgive me when I

make a mistake. God does not need to forgive me because God never judges me.

My job is to discern the root cause or trigger of my mistake. When I make the effort to understand this, then God's power can lift me above a pattern of mistake-making by boosting my discerning power. Then I can shift my behaviour, so I don't repeat the mistake.

How can someone whose loved ones are taken away from them through atrocious acts of violence believe in God's mercy?

Human beings who are involved in violence cause so much harm to others. They also cause themselves to suffer by accumulating the consequences of their negative actions. Everyone in the world has the experience of suffering.

Our collective consciousness has fallen through our attachment to the material and we have lost our power to overcome the weaknesses that control our minds and actions. Some souls are more affected by this negative energy and act on it, causing extreme harm to others.

God's mercy is to uplift me with spiritual power, so

I am no longer susceptible to weaker influences. It takes a critical mass of people to shift the collective consciousness of the world and bring all souls under a canopy of pure energy. Under God's loving guidance, this is happening now.

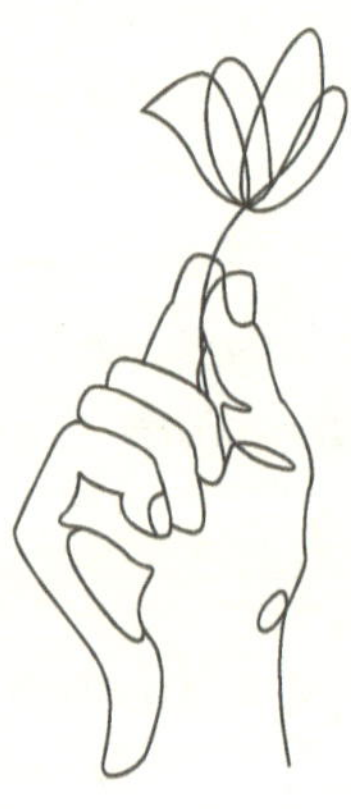

THE OCEAN OF PEACE

"My mind was full of waste thoughts, anger and criticism. Somehow God's silent waves, full of patience, gentleness and peace continued to pull me closer and closer. I felt the calmness of these Divine silent waves, playing peacefully within me. Gradually I let go of the need to be in control and just dove deep into the Ocean. I experienced a deep-rooted feeling of being safe and with an old friend of the past. Fear left."

Herdis (Disa), Iceland

The Source of Peace

Imagine being in a completely stable and changeless state, neither pulled nor pushed by any circumstances in our world but retaining a constancy of perception and being. That is how God is, and that is why God is considered an unlimited Ocean of Peace.

Peace is my own original property. God reminds me of this. The quality of God's peace and my peace is the same. The quantity, however, is different.

As my property, no one and nothing can take peace away from me unless I allow that to happen. What happens is we become dislocated from this state of peace and frantically search for it outside of ourselves.

Whereas peace for human beings may mean that there is no conflict, real peace is not the absence of something. It exists in its own right as a positive force for the reconstruction of the best that we have in this world.

We, as people, go on spiritual pilgrimages. We hold peace conferences. We even fight wars in order to protect peace.

We seek peace in nature to get away from it all. We forget that nature does not emanate peace. An afternoon on a deserted beach, a sunset seen from a majestic mountain, a walk in a virgin forest, is it peace? Or just a contrast to the great urban spreads we live in? I experience peace inside myself when I am away from my duties and responsibilities. Nature resonates with the peace that is part of my own original nature.

When the weekend or vacation in a favorite refuge finishes, we are thrown back to our regular life. From here, we contemplate the peace of nature as something far from the noise and chaos around us.

Many of us just remain at this rather wistful and disconnected level, dreaming of the next opportunity to get back to nature. We forget that peace is a state of mind and not a physical place. It is not connected with where we are or who we are with, but with how we are internally.

Because of a superficial understanding of ourselves and the things around us, any peace that we extract from our circumstances can only be ephemeral. At a surface level our minds may be jumping around here and there, but deep within the soul there is silence and peace waiting to be rediscovered and brought out into our lives.

The big waves are on the surface of an ocean. If we go skin diving just a few metres below the surface, we find a still and beautiful world. In the same way, interacting with things at a superficial level will never bring us peace. Going within, connecting with the Source of Peace will bring peace immediately.

Every time I connect with the Source of Peace, my own peace becomes activated and charged so much that it can last for hours on end. In connection with God as the Source of Peace, we can guarantee for ourselves a state of peace and equanimity that can help us through any situation.

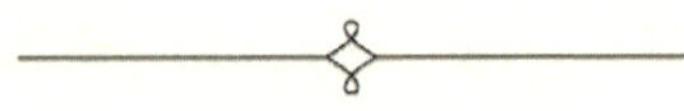

"I work in the medical field as a specialist with children. Parents are always asking me, "What did you do?" when children become very quiet and co-operative. I consider myself to be God's instrument of peace. I see medical patients as peaceful souls. Then I stop worrying what will happen to them. I just play my role helping their bodies. Meanwhile I have deep love, understanding and inner peace while with them."

Valentina, Seychelles, Africa

Personal Exploration

The essence of our being, for those who study Raja Yoga with the Brahma Kumaris, is *Om Shanti,* meaning, "I am a peaceful soul." As a being of peace, when I am *unpeaceful* or *peaceless,* I am experiencing a separation from the peaceful core of who I am.

Thich Nhat Hanh once said:

"When we can be peace, we drop feelings of us versus them and live from a place that sees no separation from others. We make peace with everyone including ourselves."

1: Let's try three experiments with peace.

- **Standing Meditation** (2 minutes)

  Stand up for a moment (as the muscle memory will invoke new experiences.) Rock back and forth on the balls of your feet for a moment. Then stand still for 2 minutes and consider what you stand for.

  Once you have an idea, stand with it as the foundation for the experience of a secure, stable, and peaceful *you* to emerge. Hold the experience and remember this feeling.

- **Walking Meditation** (3 minutes)

  Now consider a place you like to go that helps you remember your peace, where you can experience the most peaceful you. Walk around your physical space for a couple of minutes while imagining being in the peaceful place you have chosen. Hold the awareness that the peace in this place is activating the peace inside of you.

- **Sitting Meditation** (3 minutes)

  As you return to sitting, consider the wisdom you have inside that helps you face all sorts of challenges with some degree of peace. Take a moment to consider the wisdom, knowledge, realizations, or experiences you have acquired in life that help you face situations with peace. Sit contemplating this for the next few minutes and absorb the experience of peace.

2: Consider for a moment:

Is there anyone in your life you need to make peace with? Take a moment and think about how to prepare yourself mentally to make peace. Visualize what it would look like if you brought the peace inside of you into your relationship with this person.

Write down your experience to deepen it. Visualizing will help you embody this peace practically.

3: Reflection

- What stood out from these 3 short experiences?
- What do you realize about yourself as a being of peace?
- What concrete actions can you take to live from your core peace?

Take a moment to write your reflections and insights.

4: Prepare for Meditation

God is known as the Ocean of Peace. Why? This is based on an understanding that God is an unlimited source of peace, an Ocean of Peace. Prepare for meditation (page 36) then read this meditation commentary aloud and experience the Ocean of Peace.

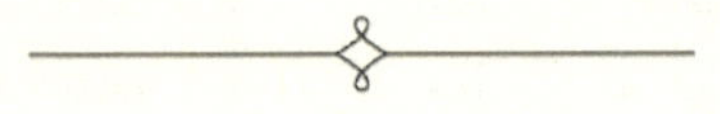

Meditation

I focus the energy of my thoughts on the point, which is the seat of my consciousness, a few centimeters behind the middle of the forehead.

I am a point of conscious energy, a point of eternal peace. As I become more stable in this consciousness, I send my thoughts to the region of spiritual light beyond this physical dimension to the home of the soul.

I become immediately aware of One who is the Supreme Source of life, the One who is eternally benevolent to all things, the one who is the Ocean of Peace.

As I come closer, I begin to understand how this Being is so pure and remains constantly positive and true, absorbed in peace.

Even though God has the knowledge of the universe and how it works and knows all of the ups and downs we've gone through on the physical stage of the play of our lives. Even so, God remains unalterably peaceful.

As the Ocean of Peace, God knows no sorrow, nor gives any pain or sorrow to other beings.

With this Divine example in front of me, I realize that I too, must become peaceful like that One.

God, You inspire me to become totally free of all selfish desires.

Just by being in Your company, I am drawn back to my original quality of peace, which I had forgotten. You gently accept me. In this acceptance, I am nurtured and healed. My heart opens to receive Your peace.

I begin a heart-to-heart conversation with You. Just by Your influence, I know that I can be what I truly am.

In my sweet, silent home and Your elevated company, I really understand the true nature of peace.

I know that this has always been my true destination and that I have finally arrived.

I absorb Your rays of peace deeply into myself. As I absorb, I am given the courage to change. I receive the faith to believe in myself once again.

I feel so much peace from You that my only wish is to allow others to be what they can be with no desire to possess or interfere.

From here, in Your company, I can make the contrast between the heartbreak and confusion of the physical world, and the experience of profound peace that You give me.

By remembering who You are, I remember who I am and what my true vocation is – to be an instrument of peace in the world.

You have gently guided me back to myself. I have awakened and my attitude and consciousness are filled with positivity.

On one side I receive this incredible infusion of Your peace, and on the other I spread it out into the world as a beacon of peace.

I remain in the joy of this consciousness for some time more, and gradually come back to my place and activities in this world.

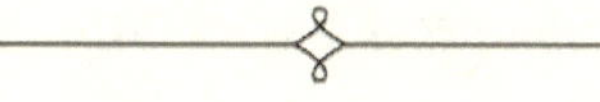

Frequently Asked Questions

My day starts with the news of violence and calamity in the world, how can God bring peace to me or the world?

When I draw peaceful energy from God, I am able to stay peaceful and not react to the stress and crisis of the world around me. In this way, I create a sense of calm, which is helpful to others. This can rekindle the experience of peace for others. God works through us as we bring this pure, peaceful energy into this world.

Being peace-less (without peace) today seems more common that peaceful. Why did God let this happen?

God, as a Being of pure peace, cannot cause the violence or peace-lessness of today's world. Nor can God stop it with a snap of the fingers. As human beings, we must rediscover our own peace again and value it so much that we let go of the ego, righteousness and anger that are causing the vengeance and violence in today's world. God, as a Beacon of Peace, is always there transmitting peace for those who begin to see its value and wish to connect. Then we bring this peace into the world with enough Divine power to create peace for all.

Anxiety is a pandemic especially among young people, they seem immune to peace. How can God help?

Many people seek the practice of meditation because of the experience of anxiety. Knowing and experiencing myself as a peaceful soul in a body living in a physical world, allows me to pull my energy away from worldly concerns and vibrations into a silence space within.

It is in this space or experience that I can connect with God. God's power of peace can make me feel like I am floating in a warm, safe ocean. Then my worries dissolve, and I am ready to face life situations with calm and confidence.

THE PROTECTOR

"God protects me from the sorrows of this world by awakening in me the awareness that I am a soul and my original nature is good, true, pure and whole. This seed of awareness was planted in my mind and grew strong enough to cut through the sorrow of my past stories. I no longer think I am missing something, lacking something or needing something from life to be complete and whole. I realise that my true roots are spiritual, and this has been a healing and a protection."

Sarah, UK

Real Protection

The world we live in has become quite dangerous. We live in the times of *suddenly* when anything can happen to anyone, anywhere, anytime. Anxiety due to an almost permanent state of uncertainty is on the rise.

If we get to such a tangled state internally, hovering around deep fears and unrequited sorrow, we realize that no one can really help us except God. We turn to God for protection, even uncertain that we will receive it.

Considering God as the protector of humanity has been one of the basic tenets of 70% of people who believe in God. Exactly how this protection is expressed is unknown to us, but we say, with blind faith "God will protect us no matter what." And we think that all we have to do is believe, praise appropriately and pray and we will be protected.

The main questions are:

- From what do we need God's protection?
- What can we do to guarantee protection?

The answer to the first question is related to the true

nature of the soul and its relationship with God, the Supreme Soul.

If, out of blind faith, we get some help from God in a moment of need, we thank the Divine. This reaffirms our faith. If, however, we don't get help, we say "It was God's will," or that it is "Divine providence" for us to carry the burden, go through the illness or difficulty. By grinning and bearing it, we postpone the understanding of how God's protection really works.

While we are not aware of our own responsibility in creating and sustaining sorrowful or difficult situations, we cannot act upon the seeds that generate them.

The first step then, is to take responsibility for our thoughts, words and actions. No one else jumps into my head to create my thoughts, no matter what the provocation. Those thoughts lead to the words and actions that generate sorrow-producing situations.

By taking responsibility for our actions, we can approach God, not as beggars or supplicants, but as willing students seeking to understand a better way. In this case, we hold the responsibility to accept the difficulty and respond with dignity and peace. Then

God carries the burden of protection.

This level of closeness is the fruit of an open and clear dialogue with God that we can call a heart-to-heart conversation. Instead of a vague sense of God's presence in our lives, there is a very real sense of being in God's company. In that remembrance, protection is guaranteed.

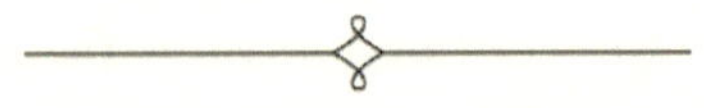

"I was walking on one of the New York streets late at night. I was a bit worried and afraid. I started remembering and talking to God as my partner and immediately got the feeling that someone was beside me and answering me. I saw a few people watching me while walking but I felt like I was under a canopy of protection. I reached the meditation center safely. I feel empowered knowing God is my protector."

Jignesh, Sweden

Personal Exploration

1: Protection is a reciprocal arrangement, not automatic. People believe that God protects automatically but in fact, it has something to do with the depth of our relationship with God that protects us. It is our relationship with God that protects us.

- Remember for a moment what it feels like when you are at your best.

- Choose three words to describe the experience of what it feels like when you are at your best.

- Take a clean sheet of paper and draw a heart at the center of the page. Write your three words inside the heart.
- Draw a circle around the heart. Consider this your *Circle of Protection*. Take a moment in silence to honour these three qualities.

- Now consider: What draws you outside of your *Circle of Protection*? Write these *pulls* outside the circle you have drawn.

- What keeps you inside the *Circle of Protection*, in touch with your best self? Write inside or around the circle of protection your answer to 2 aspects:

- What thoughts keep you safe?
- What daily practices help you stay at your best?

2: Reflection

- What does this *Circle of Protection* activity suggest to you about self-protection?
- We understand that God helps those who help themselves, what do you do to protect your best self? What more can you do?
- How do you experience the relationship of God as protector?

3: Preparing to Meditate

My qualities are the same as God's qualities, although God has these qualities to a Supreme degree.

My relationship with God is based on like-attracts-like. The qualities at the centre of me are the same as God's qualities. Prepare to meditate (page 36) then read this meditation commentary aloud and experience God's protection.

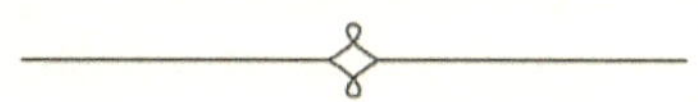

Meditation

I become aware of the soul that I am. I mentally sit on my seat of command, a little back from the middle of the forehead.

I become aware of the world around me and begin to elevate my mind, just observing what is going on. Immediately I feel a sense of control over my body and surroundings.

I go to the centre of my life and become aware of the constellation of people and objects that I am connected with.

Sitting in the centre of my life, I can see how much insecurity people go through, just because they don't know who they are as spiritual beings. They don't know from whom they can experience any sense of security.

I know how much I need a connection with the Source of all spiritual power, the one we call God, who can activate the best in me.

I know that having these qualities in a more permanent way in my life, will protect me from many things.

I know that obstacles will come, but my deep spiritual qualities that flow from my relationship with God, will help me go through them or over them with success.

I gently send myself to the region of light that is my spiritual home and the home of all souls.

On the screen of my mind I am aware of the gentle rays of spiritual light from the Source of spiritual power for all of us, God the Highest One.

I see myself in front of You, my Supreme Father and Mother and immediately feel a sense of safety, away from all confusion.

I open up to catch the rays of Your spiritual power as I focus my love on You.

As I become more stable and calm, I feel how this actually helps me and spreads to my network of roles, relationships and responsibilities.

As I become more stable, You help me come in touch with my deep, innate qualities of peace, love, contentment, truth and purity.

Your presence helps me to activate these qualities even more, so that they become more present in my life.

I become aware that the light that I receive from You becomes like a shield of protection.

In this state of loving detachment, I am still aware that there are tasks waiting for me in the many roles that I have. I know that this loving connection with You will protect me from the negative influences that may come up.

I know my default reaction will then be one of understanding, acceptance and ease.

The clarity of perception that my connection with You brings me, helps me naturally to put things in their place, understand the context and have an attitude of only giving.

I feel Your protection deeply, to the extent that I become protected from my own useless thinking.

I feel that there is a moving canopy of protection over me that will accompany me wherever I go.

In the deeper sense of security and comfort of this consciousness, I gradually come back to my daily affairs.

Frequently Asked Questions

When I am in my darkest hours, how can God protect me from myself?

My darkest moments are a result of old patterns of thoughts and feelings that get me stuck in heavy energy. When I remember God, I am choosing to look up to the light, beyond my own darkness with the understanding that the dark energy I am experiencing is like a cloud passing in front of the sun. The sun, my own inner light and God's light, is always there. When I focus on the sun, I ensure that I stay safe from dark clouds.

In times of war, women and children suffer the most. Where is God's protection then?

The tragedy of human violence is experienced most by those who cannot protect themselves physically or financially. Violence has become such a *normal* part of life that it is contagious. One act of violence provokes another until a flame of violence engulfs us all. Ego and anger are the fuel that destroys everything in its path.

In these times, another energy is needed to put out the fire of violence. Women around the world take care of homes and families with selfless love. This energy of love is a lifeline to stay connected with God. God protects a pure heart by giving it strength to face the most difficult situations. Only pure hearts can create a protection for the spirit.

It seems if I make one mistake, my whole day falls apart. Can God protect me from that one mistake every day?

When I know the common mistakes, I make every day, I can present them to God with a clean, honest heart and ask God to give me the strength and guidance to overcome them. As I draw more power from God, I notice the mistake earlier and have time to redirect myself to a better response. Slowly I become detached from the mistake.

My part is to maintain determination to free myself from mistakes. God's part is to support me with pure power.

THE LIBERATOR

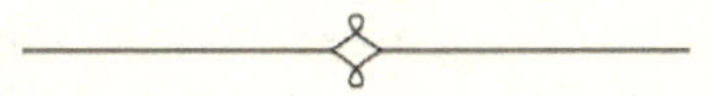

"Lack of clarity and understanding make me confused, unhappy and stressed out. Then there is a lot of overthinking and effort, yet the results do not make me happy. Clarity brings so much freedom and lightness. I experience this from God, and it makes everything easy."

Kartikeya, India

True Freedom

Freedom has two sides - freedom *from* and freedom *to*. I have to be free *from* those situations and attachments that bring me down or hold me back. I also have to be free *to* be able to express my true potential.

Looking at nature, I can get a glimpse into what freedom could mean as totally natural. Watching seagulls happily playing and gliding around, I could ask myself, "How is it that I don't feel as free as they do?"

The answer is of course, they are just being themselves. In the same way, grass grows without any effort, clouds form, rain comes and the sun shines. Nature unfolds in an inexorable symphony of ease.

Generations of people have sought peace and quiet away from the urban sprawls in their attempts to get back to nature, at least for the weekends. It is as if that nature calls to our inner nature to meet and better understand ourselves.

One of the greatest paradoxes is that freedom is part of the original nature of the soul itself. Before we come to this physical dimension, we have no thoughts and even no relationships with anyone or anything. In that sense, we are originally free. That is why there is such a yearning for a sense of spiritual freedom when we don't have it anymore.

Some even think that this world is a place of suffering and that we have to become free from the clutches of an endless wheel of rebirth. To do that, they recommend leading a morally correct life, being mindful, wise and aware in the use of our thoughts, words and actions.

Others have said that truth sets us free. It is not freedom itself that is our most precious possession, but it is the understanding of it. Being true to myself, to my deep inner qualities and to my relationship with God, will automatically show me how to remain free while doing things and interacting with others.

All of this brings us back to the basic question of "who am I?" This is the eternal teaser for questing minds. In the Koran, it says that God gave intelligence to angels and appetites to animals. And to human beings, God gave both, intelligence and appetites. This is probably exactly where we get stuck. We develop what we think is intelligence and get into all sorts of bondages. We obey our appetites and become prisoners of the objects of our senses.

Like birds holding onto the branches of trees, we pray to God to free us from whatever mess we have succeeded in creating for ourselves. The Divine looks back at us and says, "The branches are not holding onto you, you are holding onto them."

God is seen by many as the ultimate Liberator, the One who holds the key to the lock on our intellects. This means that the Supreme doesn't just open the cage and let me out, God explains very clearly who I am, what my qualities are and what I can do. This frees me to be who I really am.

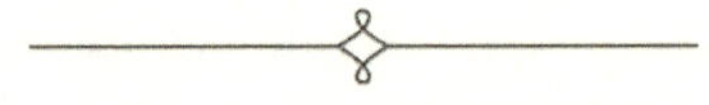

"Sometimes I experience dark moments and feel trapped. Then I feed my mind with lots of junk food thoughts that make chaos and problems in my mental digestion. I became more reactive with people. This never-ending negative cycle is broken when I experience God's pure energy. It empowers me by bringing clarity into my mind. This light and lovely feeling of completeness enlarges my inner capacity and opens me up to the unlimited best in me."

Mona, Indonesia.

Personal Exploration

1: Take a moment and imagine your complete and perfect self, an embodiment of your highest aspiration. Visualize yourself as complete and whole.

- How would it feel? What would be the experience of this completeness, this wholeness?

2: With this image firmly in your mind, think about the barriers or obstacles you are experiencing now that stop you from being your best, e.g. a pattern of thoughts or feelings, a negative behaviour or habit.

3: Take 3-4 strips of paper (2 inches wide) and write each obstacle in big letters on one strip of paper. Staple or tape the first slip of paper to make a circle, then create a chain by looping the other slips of paper (stapled or taped) together. Once all the obstacles are attached as a paper chain and it loops back connecting the first and last loop, call it *the Chain that Limits Me from being who I truly am.*

4: Now consider: What does the word *chain* suggest to you? What are the positive and negative connotations of the word?

Whatever the connotation, a chain can constrain me, so I lose my freedom. We must loosen or remove these chains in order to be free. How?

5: Consider these two cycles. On a piece of paper draw the two cycles with arrows connecting each point:

- **Vicious Cycle -** Negative thoughts lead to feeling bad - which lead to saying negative things - which leads to acting in ways that hurt myself or others - which lead to negative thoughts.

- **Virtuous Cycle -** Positive thoughts lead to feeling good - which leads to speaking well of others - which leads to actions that uplift myself and others - which lead to positive thoughts.

Our chain of obstacles is like a vicious cycle. We can break out of the *Vicious Cycle* anywhere to begin a *Virtuous Cycle.* This is what liberation is about, breaking the chain of vicious cycles to be free.

6: God's role is to fill us with the power required to break vicious cycles. We can learn to overcome negativity by raising our gaze above the obstacles to access a pure energy that empowers and clarifies. It is my thoughts that create the chains that bind me. By changing my thoughts, I can change the cycle.

7: Look at the *Chain that Limits Me* and consider where you can break into this vicious cycle to create a virtuous cycle for yourself. Find the link in the chain that can be broken. Consider how to change it then break the chain by ripping the paper apart. Rewrite the links to create a virtuous cycle for yourself.

8: Reflection

- What was most helpful to you in this exercise?
- What does this activity suggest to you about liberation?
- What insights do you have about God's role in liberation?

9: Pick a strategy to use in one area of your life to liberate yourself from a place where you feel caught in a vicious cycle.

10: Prepare for Meditation (page 36) then enjoy reading this meditation commentary aloud. Sit in silence to absorb the energy. Then listen to a beautiful song (suggestion: *Be Who You Were Born to Be* by Bliss.)

Meditation

I gently go into the awareness of being the spiritual entity giving life to this physical body.

I am a tiny point of conscious energy sitting on my seat of command behind the middle of the forehead.

At this moment, I'm in the centre of everything that is going on around me, my life and the lives of others.

Since I am calm and stable in the centre, I can feel my peace.

Since I am not running after things mentally, I feel my deep contentment.

Since I am feeling very still, I am aware of my basic nature of love towards everything and everyone.

As a soul, I existed before this physical body and will continue after it dies. Just this consciousness reminds me of a deep sense of freedom.

Though I am aware of the world going on around me, I send my thoughts to the dimension of light beyond this physical universe, to my sweet eternal home.
On the screen of my mind, I visualize the Divine Source, the One we call by different names as God.

I come in front of that One and feel the strength that comes in these Divine rays.

I begin a loving conversation with God about freedom. You are eternally free because You know the secrets behind the creation.

You lend me Your vision so that I can feel the depth of those secrets also.

Sitting mentally with You, I become an observer of the stage where I play different roles in the physical world.

I can now understand how the real and eternal being that I am, had become caught up in the consequences of thoughts, words and actions, that came up in the course of playing these many roles.

You fill my heart with the deepest love towards the people and objects that are part of these roles in the physical world.

Because of that love, I am free from the need to be connected with other individuals and things.

I become totally light in both senses – illuminated with the light of understanding and weightless because nothing is holding me down.

In Your company I feel totally liberated from even thinking about roles and activities. You make me feel free from all burden and waste.

I feel a wonderful balance between being loving and detached which is the essence of freedom.

You fill me with so much spiritual power that I am free to serve selflessly. From this elevated state I can send pure liberating vibrations to everyone and everything that is connected with me.

Knowing that I can come back to this loving and liberating connection whenever I want, I gradually come back to the activity of the physical world.

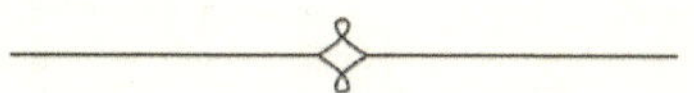

Frequently Asked Questions

How can God liberate anyone from the sorrow and darkness of these times?

Darkness is an absence of light. I cannot chase away the darkness in my mind or in the world. But I can introduce more and more light. When I turn my attention towards the beauty, purity and peace of God's light, I find myself becoming lighter. Then, instead of interacting with darkness, I stay focused on the light. When focused on staying light, there is no mental space to get drawn into darkness. I am aware it is there, but I am not attracted to it and I do not get lost in it.

Why does God not hear the cries of the innocent ones trapped in horrible situations? Why doesn't God free them from their misery?

There is so much anger and violence in the world today that these distressing vibrations affect us all. Some people will act on this energy and do horrible things.

When we go through difficult situations in life, we have the habit of attributing the bad things to God. When I think that the Divine has given me the good things in my life, then I can also believe that God has given me the negative. What if God does neither? What if my choices and actions bring me both the good and the bad in my life?

God's role is to constantly give me the energy and support to make good choices and face the consequences of my bad choices in a dignified way. When horrible things happen, God is always there giving strength, love, courage and hope to help me through.

Can God help free people from the addictions and harmful behaviours that plague them today?

Addictions come when I feel empty and the emptiness is more than I can bear. Then I look to fill the emptiness with something else such as self-medicating with drugs or alcohol, television, shopping or simply getting lost in anything that takes my mind away from my inner suffering.

The wounds and hurts from the past linger in the soul over time and must be healed. Only God's pure energy can unearth the deep roots of past pain and dissolve them in the light of love. Healing is liberating. Spending time in God's love-full light begins to dissolve the wounds that bind me in destructive behaviours.

SOURCE OF POWER

"Sometimes the demands of job and family responsibilities make me feel powerless. When I look to God as my Source of Power, there is nothing I can't solve. Imagining I am just God's executive assistant lightens my feeling of heaviness and gives me the power to execute daily tasks with more efficiency and accuracy. God has given me the strength to easily overcome my weaknesses and negative habits. I draw Power from God and become more stable in the events of my life."

Murli, Malaysia

The Powers of God

There is a lot of confusion about what God does and does not do. Even though human beings, across the spectrum of religions, state that God is unknowable, many say categorically that the Supreme is also omnipresent, omnipotent and omniscient. For this, God receives the title of Almighty.

Because God is a soul like us - albeit Supreme - we can interact with God in the highest form of every relationship.

God is not a diffused or impersonal energy, but a resident of the home of subtle light beyond the physical universe, referred to as Heaven, Nirvana, the soul world, the supreme abode and so on. Just as the physical sun is in one place and radiates light to the whole solar system, God remains in that spiritual dimension and shines light on all. Because of this, I can immediately direct my thoughts to the Divine and begin a loving interaction.

The expression, "O God, wherever I am, You are with me" expresses a poetic closeness. It doesn't mean that God is literally present everywhere, in the pebbles and stones, you, me and everything.

God is a spiritual sun of perfect attributes. The sense of closeness that I have with the Supreme is beyond physical dimensions. God is only one thought away from me.

If the presence of God is misunderstood, the Almighty's powers are more so. If we believe that God is present in every single thing and person, it follows that we can believe that God directs nature and our lives.

We forget that nature has its own physical, chemical and biological laws, that function automatically without need of any Divine intervention. Even though everything is threaded together in such a wonderful way, it doesn't mean that everything is being moved by God.

There are natural interactions between souls with each other and with matter. Floods, earthquakes, droughts and volcanic eruptions are part of that interaction. They have nothing to do with what is termed the *Will of God*. They are part of the law of cause and effect between human beings and our environment.

The good and the bad things that happen to us are neither God's blessings, nor lack of them. They are the return of our own deeds.

The One who my heart tells me is the Ocean of Love would only manifest love. This One is not involved in the weakening or death of human beings. God does not make the grass grow or the wind blow or bind the energy of the atoms together. The Divine does not deal out our respective roles - this one will take birth in the streets of Calcutta, this other one will take birth in the royal family of Spain.

It is a contradiction that in spirt of not knowing what God is or does, we insist on blaming the Almighty for all things that happen beyond our comprehension. Paradoxically, when something major happens, we say, "It is God's will" and at the same time we seek God out in the temples, churches and mosques to beg for Divine favour.

God's greatness is not due to intervening in events on earth but in using spiritual power for the benefit of world transformation. In the same way that God's presence is spiritual, Divine power is purely spiritual. What can extreme love, extreme peace and extreme happiness *not* achieve?

God knows the whole process and the conditions through which things pass. Nature takes care of the details of nature and the law of cause and effect (karma) takes care of the details of human life. God knows and accepts that everything that happens is part of an eternal drama. God did not create this drama but in it, God plays the role of the Source of Spiritual Power for all human souls. By absorbing that spiritual power, souls can transform themselves and thereby help transform the world.

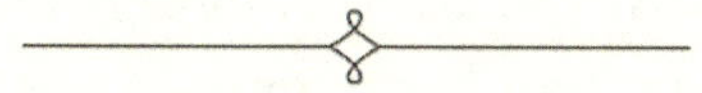

"I have experienced that my weak thoughts are powerful and bad thoughts can also come true. I remind myself that I am a child of God, the Supremely Powerful Almighty Authority. When I turn myself towards the Source, everything is possible, and nothing is impossible! God's power lifts me to a positive, clear and extremely benevolent stage."

Natasha, Ukraine

Personal Exploration

1: Take a moment and remember a time when you felt powerful. Reflect on the experience and write about the event or share with another person.

While reflecting consider:

- What conditions supported this experience of feeling powerful?
- What was the source of this power? (Could be focus, determination, pure intention, doing something I love, confidence, competence, doing something I am good at, etc.)

2: Explore the meaning of *power* as it is used in the world. It is also used in a spiritual context. What does power mean to you?

- Make two columns on a sheet of paper. At the top of one column write the title *Worldly Power,* and at the top of the other write *Spiritual Power.*
- In the first column, identify words to describe power as used and understood in the world today.
- In the other column, identify words to describe spiritual or inner power.

Consider: what is the difference between the two forms of power? How do you experience the difference between them?

Having considered these two meanings of power take a moment to consider:

- Where do you get your power from?
- What is your source of power?

3: Take a piece of paper and around the edges write down 10 aspects of your life (relationships, roles and possessions) that are important to you. Then draw yourself in the middle.

4: God is the Source of one kind of power but not the other. Spiritual power is energy to recharge the soul, like a discharged battery that requires a power boost.

Prepare for meditation (page 36) and read the meditation commentary (see next page) aloud to yourself slowly experiencing each step. Then close your eyes and hold a connection to God, the Power Source.

5: Holding the spiritual power you accumulated during the meditation, look at the piece of paper and visualize giving spiritual power through your eyes to each aspect of your life. This is a method of using God's energy through your focused thoughts to empower your life.

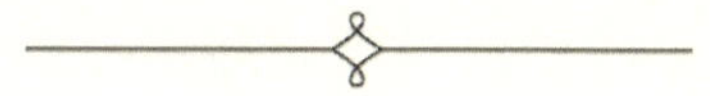

Meditation

I sit quietly and turn my mind inwards.
I become aware of my spiritual identity as a soul, a spark of infinitesimal energy, a wondrous being of light, behind the center of the forehead, looking through the eyes.

Sitting on this seat of command, I become aware of the things that I have accumulated over my life in terms of relationships, positions and possessions.

From this point of stillness, I observe the things of my life, this body and my thoughts and memories. I realize, this is not who I am. All this I have called mine, but it is not me.

Just being able to separate myself from everything I have accumulated, gives me a sense of understanding, responsibility and command.

This awareness is the seat of self-sovereignty and power over my life. When I look at my hand, I have control over the movement of each finger. In the same way, I have power over my mind. I am the one who creates my thoughts and feelings, no one else.

Silently and gently, I lift my awareness beyond the physical world – the senses, experiences, sounds and actions. I take myself to a region of pure, golden red light, my eternal home. Deep silence embraces me.

I gently turn my thoughts to the One we call the Almighty. I see the One as a subtle sun-like Being, just radiating power in the form of peace, love, joy, purity, truth.
I spend time with each of these qualities as I plug into the Source of Spiritual Power. I feel how God's peace empowers me.

I feel how God's Love empowers me.
I feel how God's Joy empowers me.
I feel how god's Purity empowers me.
I feel how God's Truth empowers me.

In this divine union between the soul and the Supreme, falsehood cracks and falls away, and the soul returns to its natural essence. I am connected with the Source of Spiritual Power and now comprehend the real depth of the Almighty.

God is not just a Source of Powers and Qualities but also the essence all relationships. The perfect Mother, Father, Teacher, Guide and Friend.

With a feeling of great love and humility. I consider and explore the depth of each of these relationships and how they empower me. I feel how as my Mother, God empowers me.

I feel how as my Father, God empowers me.
I feel how as my Teacher, God empowers me.
I feel how as my Guide, God empowers me.
I feel how as my Friend, God empowers me.

I remain in the bliss of this connection and relationship and gradually come back to the normality of my surroundings. The connection with the eternal Home of Light remains, the companionship with the Powerful

One remains, so that I can keep God with me during my activities. I feel totally empowered to live my life in the best way possible.

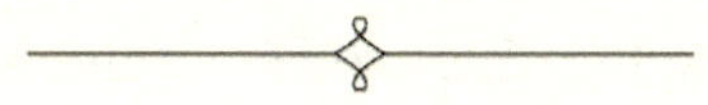

Frequently Asked Questions

What does God's power look like? How is it different than how people think about power today?

We cannot see power (either physical or spiritual) but we can see and feel the effect of power. God's power creates an energetic shift in the soul. From being stuck or heavy in a negative feeling, a person feels something moving in the spirit, like a weight being lifted. Sometimes God's power is experienced in the form of an insight or feeling of strength and clarity. It is different for each of us. This is the joy of a relationship with God, to watch for the subtle ways in which God's power uplifts and strengthens me.

Sometimes when I am at my best, I get a surge of enthusiasm and tirelessness. Is this a gift of God's power?

Yes. When I am at my best, I am vibrating at my highest frequency. This puts me directly into the energy field of God's highest vibration. It is as if we are resonating together which amplifies my highest vibration, and I feel an extra surge of energy.

It is hard to witness the suffering of others. It can make us feel helpless and afraid. As a caring human being, I want to do something. I can always give good energy.

When I hear a siren or read a terrible headline, I can immediately send thoughts of power and peace to the people involved. With this action, I am reaching out with love, I am doing something by sending good vibrations. When I give love and peace, I also protect myself from absorbing the suffering and fear around me.

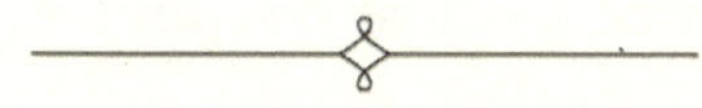

"My energy level drops with hopeless thoughts and I become weak. God is always there. My part is to go to God, to get the power I need to shift from hopeless to hopeful. Then I can bring the energy of hope to others. "When I go inside, I experience an ocean of light and silence and ego disappears. To feel myself very deep in inner silence, I can hear God's heart. This gives me stability and power to jump and fly."

Nonie, Peru

CONTINUING THE CONNECTION

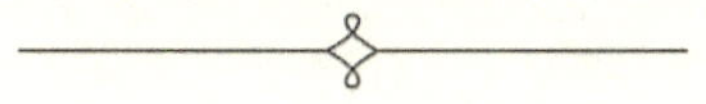

The Supreme Being has been surrounded with so much mystery that we have created a distance between ourselves and the Ultimate Source.

We now know that we can connect and enjoy the power and the qualities that emanate from God, anytime we want. It is our right to experience the wonder of having a direct link with God.

The reward of this close relationship is a more stable consciousness with which to observe the chaos of the world around us and remain unaffected by it.

After going deeply into the different practices and meditations, we hope that you are feeling that it is not so difficult after all to have a real and meaningful relationship with God.

Perhaps you have had experiences like those shared by our young meditators in this book.

"I felt God seeing me as I really am ... Tears of love ran from my eyes and I felt completely safe and secure."

"... feeling like a child belonging to the Ocean of Love (God) ... acted as an engine that gave me so much power that I could easily let go of attachment and expectations in my relationships."

"God's beam of healing light frees me from comparison ... I am free to let go of various arguments and let life take its wise course."

"God's silent waves, full of patience, gentleness and peace and give me a deep-rooted feeling of being safe and with an old friend. Fear left."

"God as my source of power solve ... whenever I have doubt, I consult God, and this makes me easy and light ... I draw Power from the Source and become more stable in the events of my life."

"I remind myself that I am the child of God ... I turn myself towards my Almighty Father, whose powerful hands take me to a

stage of positivity, clearness and extremely benevolent state."

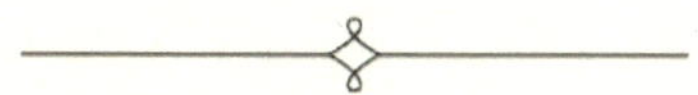

If there are any of the relationships with God that you would like to explore further, revisit the pertinent chapter regularly or continue your exploration in other ways.

We hope you have enjoyed the book as much as we enjoyed writing it. Thank you for joining us in this exploration of God. We wish you the very best on your continued journey.

Thank you to all who contributed.

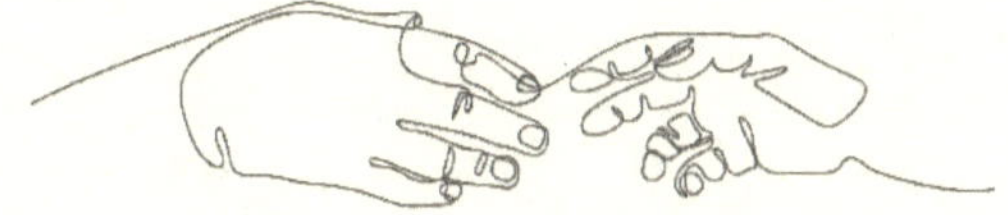

Basic Steps of Raja Yoga Meditation

We include here some of the basic steps of the Raja Yoga practice, which have been the basis of the meditations in this book. Feel free to use this as the basis for or to augment your meditation practice. By going through these steps from time to time, you will enhance your capacity and deepen your experience of meditation. Stay with each practice until you feel you have mastered it.

By going through these steps from time to time, you will enhance your capacity and deepen your experience of meditation.

Stay with each practice until you feel you have mastered it.

1. Centering in the present

Sit with your eyes slightly open. Become aware of the world around you. Listen to the sounds you can hear. Perceive the colors and forms. Feel the air as you breathe in and out. Feel that you are in the center of the 360° of activities around you. The past has finished, and the future hasn't happened yet.

You are literally in the present moment. The present is the only real time you have. Enjoy it for a few moments without thinking too much. Just have full attention on what is happening around you.

2. Centering in soul consciousness

Just as you are sitting on your seat physically, imagine a subtle seat behind the eyes, a few centimeters back from the spot between your brows. This is the seat where the conscious energy or soul sits. All thoughts, feelings, desires and ideas, as well as sensations from the body come to this point to be processed.

Sitting on this subtle seat you appreciate and decide about the direction you want to take. Spend a few minutes in this awareness of being the soul working through the physical body. Enjoy the sense of command this gives you.

3. In the center of your life

As a spiritual being, you are not only in the center of everything that is happening around you, but you are in the center of your life. There is a network of roles, relationships and responsibilities which spread out from you.

You are connected through them to people, objects and situations. Just as the center of a circle doesn't move, you are still and calm in the center of your life and activities. As you become calm, this has an immediate effect on everything that is connected to you.

Without moving internally, enjoy serving your whole network with peaceful vibrations. Be aware that you are the creator of the reality of your life.

4. Experiencing your eternity

Become centered in the consciousness of being the soul in the body. Observe the physical world around you without thinking too much. Observe the present situations in which you find yourself, as if you are watching the scenes of a film. As a spiritual being going through a human experience, be aware that at some point in the past, you came into this physical body when it was still in the womb of your mother.

You were born, grew up, and went through many experiences and now you are meditating on your true nature. At some point in the future, you, the soul will leave this body and continue on your journey. This life then becomes a chapter of a book. You are the energy that gives life to the whole book and not just to this chapter. You are the conscious energy that continues. You have come from forever. You will continue forever. Because you do not have any size or physical dimension, nothing can destroy you. You are eternal. Stay in this consciousness for a few minutes.

5. The inner state of peace, love and happiness

When you are in a state of rest as described above, you have a chance to experience the deeper qualities which are innate in the soul. Become the detached observer and experience that, when you are still, there is the natural experience of peace, love and happiness.

These are qualities which have always been in the soul. As we move from one life to the next (or one chapter to the next), many things are recorded on top of these original qualities. With time, we forget them.

They become buried by momentary desires and considerations. Since you have gone back to your inner center, you can now appreciate the difference between what you really are deeply and what you have become at this time in your life. Remain a few minutes in this deep state of spiritual enjoyment.

6. Connection with God, the Source of spiritual power

As a soul, you are not made of material energy. Your existence is in another dimension as well. There is a dimension of subtle light beyond this physical universe, that the different religious traditions call heaven, nirvana or simply, the home of souls. The One who we call God also resides there. We try to reconnect with that One in prayer.

As you become centered in soul consciousness and aware of your innate qualities of peace, love and happiness, you gradually move away from the physical dimension and become a silent observer. Internally, you become aware of this dimension of light and come closer to that One who is like a subtle sun, radiating spiritual power.

Mentally, visualize the meeting between the soul and God. Open yourself to receive the rays of that spiritual power. You will feel as if your battery is being recharged, that your love, peace and happiness are really being activated. Stay in that state of deep appreciation of your connection with the Source, for a few more minutes.

7. Relationships with God

That One, is not only the Source of spiritual power, but is also the essence of all relationships. Become centered in soul consciousness and mentally connected with God, as in the previous exercise. Start a conversation with the One in any one of the relationships that you consider important.

God is the Mother, Father, Teacher, Guide, Friend, Beloved and so on. Imagine that the connection between you and God revolves around that relationship. Initiate and continue a conversation for as long as you want from your side as the child, student, follower, friend, lover and so on. Leave yourself open for the answers that come to you in each conversation.

Remain in this loving interchange for a few minutes and come back recharged and ready to face the situations of your life.

Visit a Brahma Kumaris meditation centre in your area at: www.brahmakumaris.org

www.ingramcontent.com/pod-product-compliance
Lightning Source LLC
LaVergne TN
LVHW091049150826
845673LV00002B/514

* 9 7 9 8 8 9 6 3 2 0 5 8 6 *